STOP!
You're Killing the Business

STOP!

YOU'RE KILLING

THE BUSINESS

Howard J. Klein

Mason & Lipscomb PUBLISHERS   NEW YORK

COPYRIGHT © 1974 *by* Howard J. Klein

All rights reserved

No part of this book may be reproduced in any form without permission in
writing from the publisher

ISBN: 0–88405–060–2

Library of Congress Catalog Card Number: 73–92445

Printed in the United States of America

FIRST PRINTING

Library of Congress Cataloging in Publication Data

Klein, Howard J   1935–
  Stop! You're killing the business.
  I. Small business—Management—Case studies.
I. Title.   II. Title: You're killing the business.
HD69.S6K567   658′.022   73–92445
ISBN 0–88405–060–2

Contents

Introduction

R U N N I N G a business is a tough job. Sophisticated business schools will teach you about bottom lines, synergism, and profit centers, but all this technical knowledge can't prevent a man from making a damn fool out of himself if he's got a mind to do it. You don't need an M.B.A. from the Harvard Business School to know the one thing that every businessman needs to know more than anything else: how not to be an idiot. Everybody knows that competition, or underfinancing, or outworn ideas, or neglect will kill any business. But objective as you may like to think you are, you probably will never admit the truth of the immortal admonition of Pogo: "We have met the enemy and he is us."

Few businessmen will admit to having made disastrous errors in judgment. That's why they hire particularly loyal people —not for the sake of that abstract quality, but primarily to have people around them on whom they can shunt the blame. That's why they love to find outside forces for business failure—from bad weather to political instability. After all, it's not their fault that this year's inventory of sunglasses didn't sell because it rained all summer.

The ten murder stories here represent the most instructive cases illustrating man's inhumanity to his business. They are histories of privately or family owned companies, or small, publicly held companies of recent vintage. In all cases, operating control was in the hands of the founder or his surrogates. These were small growing businesses with strong forward momentum, grossing $1 million or more in annual sales but less than $10 million.

There are, you will see, many congenital personality faults rooted in the failure stories in this book, and you may gain the impression that there was little the principal characters could have done to stave off the killing. After 3 years of research, I've concluded otherwise.

Why would any enlightened man consciously commit corporate murder by attributing everything that went wrong to things like "bum luck" or "getting screwed"?

I've set out to answer the question by examining cases of people in the process of murdering businesses. I've studiously avoided any endeavor to compile an overpowering list of statistics to show why small businesses fail. Too many people who read such figures go broke anyway. My own "statistics" are elementary:

1] One hundred per cent of the time, self-serving stupidity, egoism, jealousy, and greed running amuck in your business can cripple it badly, but all alone, they can't kill it.

2] Businesses reaching sales of $1 million a year or more can double in sales every 5 years if they are wisely (I said wisely, not necessarily brilliantly) managed. This is true 99% of the time.

And yet, I've witnessed countless murders which could have been prevented by common sense. I've seen the work of 30 years tumble to ashes in months. I can't remember how many times during the last 15 years I've listened to the forlorn lamentations of small business employees who comment on the destruction of a company with anguished exclamations like: "Oh God, how Jack would be turning over in his goddamn grave if he saw what these dummies were doing to his business now . . ."

I've had the feeling too. You can almost feel a tremor beneath the floor. As if someone downstairs is banging up from the basement with a broomstick thundering to all of us: "Stop! Stop, you stupid bastards, you're killing my business!"

1

How to Kill the Family Business *or* Do You Sincerely Want to Murder Your Brother-in-Law

S I N C E early childhood, walking the streets of New York, I've been continuously enchanted by the proud name of a Moving and Storage Company called THE SEVEN SANTINI BROTHERS. I cannot imagine a real company that has seven brothers working in it. Family businesses I've been familiar with have proved managerial torture chambers with two brothers. I know two brothers who really sent each other to early graves over business quarrels. One guy killed the other out of sheer stubbornness, and the deceased brother's widow then proceeded to aggravate the survivor to death with unending accusations of guilt for his brother's death.

I don't know much about the Seven Santini Brothers and I'm unwilling to rupture my fantasy which lingers on by interviewing them and maybe learning they really do hate each other's guts. But two brothers or seven, three sons-in-law or one daughter-in-law, I've studied a few family businesses and can report most are ripe for destruction because the principals in the business generally can't recognize what I call the Deadly Triangle. There are several versions:

Father, Son, Son-in-Law
Father, Son, Son
Brother, Brother, Nephew

These deadly combinations of blood are tough enough to manage during Grandpa's 8oth birthday party. Imagine how they possess the power to kill growing companies.

Lest we be accused of incurable cynicism, let's state our belief that family businesses can work. Family business associates can be tolerant of each others' failings, proud of each others' triumphs, sensitive to one another's ego needs, and share a sense of building something worthwhile to everyone's benefit. But these are exceptions; let's look at the rule.

The most lethal of all Deadly Triangles is the Father–Son–Son-in-Law variety and the subject of our narrative.

The germinal figure of our story is a man named Randolph G. Cates, who established a wholesale hardware supply firm just prior to World War I. He came from a Fundamentalist family in the South, bringing North with him that singular rectitude and purposefulness that so often accompanies great success. His wife bestowed upon him four healthy sons and, as each came of age, they joined the business because it was natural that they do so.

Cates General Hardware Supply Company grew vigorously with the nation and the economy over the next twenty years. By the mid-1930's, the firm was supporting the father, his four sons, and their growing families in reasonable comfort.

It was during this time, when the company was inching its way out of the Great Depression relatively unscathed and slowly expanding, that the challenge arrived. Randolph began to sense a new, disturbing element intruding among the relationships of his sons: petty jealousies. His four sons, who loved each other deeply, began playing against each other for their father's favor. Randolph, a devout, church-going man, who had worked to forge an iron bond of love between his sons, was sick at heart, but he perceived the cold realities and sensed what he now had to do.

Without warning, Randolph Cates announced he was selling the company to a larger competitor. The proceeds of the sale were to be divided equally four ways. This inexplicable act shocked and saddened his sons. They begged him to reconsider. Father Cates was immovable. Each now had 25% of the equity in the firm in cash, and each could now decide either to pool his share with another brother or go off on his own. Randolph would not decide. He left his stunned brood and went to California.

Whether Randolph's judgment was good or bad is an issue for another discussion. But it now set the stage for a much larger drama that was yet to unfold.

The Cates brothers decided to split, and each established

a small hardware wholesaling business. World War II brought changes, and the prosperous postwar period saw them establishing themselves successfully in different fields. Jack Cates was now the only one of the four original brothers who was still in the wholesale hardware business. He proudly carried on the family tradition and named his company R. & J. Cates & Sons. Jack's son, Michael, was literally raised in the company, squatting on his father's desk or playing among the dusty bins of nails. He had the calling loud and clear. He loved the give and take, the arguing, the play of husky truck drivers, the latest sexy jokes he found every day at the "place"—as the company came to be known.

So the curious skein continued. Michael Cates graduated in 1958 from Eastern University and the following day exchanged his cap and gown for a sweatshirt and dirty jeans without the least thought of "interviewing" or doing the job thing. He was a man with a superb college education delivering a rush order of hand tools. In those days of "silent generation," button-down minds, it did not at all seem incongruous to Michael that a man's education had nothing to do with whether he wanted to display it in the board room or on the delivery van.

Michael was working and dreaming toward the future. He had no rivals among his cousins. And nature had given him a sweet little sister whose only thoughts were who was the cutest boy at Central High.

There was no way that anyone or anything would stand in the way of Michael Cates and his burning charge up the hill. Every thought, every instinct, and every impulse within him was now directed toward the increasing prosperity of R. & J. Cates & Sons. Urged and encouraged both by his father and aging grandfather, Michael assumed a sense of command and presence in the family that he was the lone star bringing the grand tradition of Cates into a new world.

After a brief but active bachelor life of about 3 years, Michael met Susan Bellows during a trip to England. Susan came from a modest home where her father worked for the Department of Labor as a statistician. They were married in 1962 and began, almost at once, a prolific production of another generation. He was a young man in a hurry.

During this time, Michael's sister, Jennifer, had completed her 3 years of college with no immediate prospects in sight. At a time when most of her contemporaries were already sporting fraternity pins on their bulging bosoms or engagment rings on their pudgy fingers, the charming Jennifer Cates lived in an insular world of ski weekends, sorority teas, dances, and Ivy League romances. Jack and Helen Cates worried about their baby. Being popular and the cheer leader that every Saturday network television camera picked up at State U. football games was wonderful. Yet Jenny seemed to feel it could go on forever. Jack, above all, wanted to protect his daughter from a cold flop on hard pavement should she graduate the following year without an immediately suitable young man in tow.

There followed a series of country club romances—encouraged by her parents—which broke to bits Jenny's remaining illusions about playing Scarlet O'Hara for the rest of her life. Graduation was drawing near. She presented the alternatives to her nervous parents. She would either go to New York to study acting or join the Peace Corps. Neither of these noble pursuits appealed to the Cateses at all. Jack was prepared to stop Jenny at all costs, yet he could not bring himself to demand she stay around home waiting for Rhett Butler to show up. So he decided to send her on a trip to Europe for a new perspective.

A month before the proposed trip, Jenny visited the local travel agency. As she chatted with the owner about the Palazzo Vecchio, her eye caught a lean, handsome young man sitting at the back desk scribbling on long sheets of accounting papers. He looked up and instantly recognized her. They'd been classmates in Comparative American Music, a crap course at State. Frank walked over and re-introduced himself. They went out for a drink together shaking with laughter about the bumbling incompetent who had attempted to teach 17 seniors about a subject in which they had no interest. Jenny and Frank Talbot started dating.

The romance heated up so fast that Jenny cut her trip short and flew home to be Frank's date for an alumni dance that September. Frank had enjoyed Jenny's gaiety, her good looks, and trim figure. His ardor raced even more, however, when his well-tutored accountant's eye began to discern the presence of assets more substantial than the modest, ranch-style Cates home suggested.

Frank was no fortune hunter. He was an honest, pleasant, likeable young man who had good sense. But he was also a young man from a working-class home who sensed his own limitations. He realized, after a few short months at the accounting firm, that one could never grow rich explaining deductions to travel agents. The sensible alternative was to marry a rich girl, but unwilling to compromise himself, he was prepared to wait until he found a rich girl he could love. It appeared that Jenny was that girl.

As Frank and Jenny's courtship grew into the talking turkey stage, the Cateses deployed all the customary wiles at their command to entice him more quickly into their golden web. Jack took Frank to his bustling warehouse and proudly pointed to the stacks of merchandise. He'd walk him around the yard showing off the ten trucks proudly emblazoned with the Cates logo. Frank happily obliged his future father-in-law by acting deeply impressed and then he and Jenny laughed, hugged, kissed, and screwed their way through a year-long engagement at the end of which was one of the biggest weddings the town had seen since Michael Cates had married Susan Bellows.

Michael, meanwhile, happily contemplating the prospect of his kid sister marrying a nice accountant, began moving the company into a new activity his father had never contemplated. He decided to establish Cates in the commercial hardware field by bidding on large construction contracts. The week Frank and Jenny were married, Michael wrote the first big commercial contract in the firm's history. It was for $50,000. Once again, the world opened wide for the lucky Cateses.

As the company began its big climb, a problem suddenly appeared in the happy new nest of Frank and Jennifer Cates Talbot. Frank earned a decent beginner's wage at his accounting firm. The three partners liked his work, his integrity, and his rosy outlook. The clients liked him because he always seemed to have extra time for them. He was a young man who did things precisely and had an old-fashioned sense of fair play. He correctly assessed his situation. He was embarked on a long, tedious journey in business life whose greatest reward could be a partnership in an accounting firm in a small midwestern city. That went against his grain, but he didn't brood about it. He was too busy having a good time playing the young married.

Jenny wasn't so sanguine. She was too accustomed to having too much. She'd always had plenty of folding money at her fingertips to indulge her smallest whim. Observing sister-in-law Susan's rampant spending sprees which had grown out of Michael's hard-won success in the business, Jenny grew petulant. Here was Susan, a civil service worker's daughter, moving into a massive house on the hill, ordering around servants, gorging herself on clothes, jewels, trips, and country club memberships, and she, Jennifer, the golden girl of State U. was playing cutesy *I Love Lucy*, circa 1956, in a "darling little three-room apartment." Darling, my ass, Jenny thought, this crap has got to stop.

One day she telephoned her father at the company and asked him to meet her at a quiet restaurant at the other end of the city. Jack immediately drove over. At first, he feared some terrible news about Jenny's marriage. Then she presented her list of demands in her best daddy's-little-girl way. Jack naturally melted. What kind of idiot had he been? Hadn't he realized that Frank's pride was standing in the way of his daughter's happiness? No goddamn daughter-in-law was going to live like a fairy princess while his baby played the Little Match Girl.

The following month, Frank Talbot was brought into R. & J. Cates & Sons as assistant office manager to train for General Office Manager until the present man could comfortably be made to retire early. Then quickly, Frank assumed full control of the office, of credit, and general operations. Six months later his income had tripled; he drove a sleek, new luxury sedan, moved to a newer apartment, and flew for two weeks to Hawaii with Jenny. The cutesy days were over.

Thus the deadly triangle was forged in the crucible of a father's love.

At first, the filial problems were minimal. The three men maintained a pleasant, casual, even sportive relationship. They lunched together almost every day, belonged to the same downtown athletic club, went to ball games together on warm afternoons, and hunted together in winter. Jack Cates had enough good sense to ease potential friction by separating managerial functions as much as he could see possible. Inevitably, however, friction, as it must, began to erode this happy trio.

It began innocently enough. Frank was a tenacious credit man. His overzealous collection techniques seemed abrasive to many old-line customers who were slow payers. Every small business has them. The slow payers whose credit is good as gold but who survive year to year by the strategy of using O.P.M. (other people's money). Frank refused to enjoy the nostalgia often proffered in place of checks and pressed hard for his money. He began really leaning on a few old-timers by refusing to ship their orders.

The mechanical confirmation of Frank's mind tolerated no such small-business traditions. Why, he reasoned, should these bums sit on our dough for 120 days? Because they always pay anyway? Because they had bought from his grandfather-in-law? Because they knew his father-in-law when he delivered plugs? No dice. Pay up or no goods. Look at the burgeoning business Michael was doing with big contractors. Who the hell needed these small retailers anymore?

Jack Cates needed them, or so he was convinced. He continued to politely remind Frank that servicing small retail hardware stores still comprised the bulk of the Cates business. This weak admonition was forgotten soon enough because, the very next day, Frank telephoned an old lumber yard account and laced into the owner over a 90-day-old invoice. He told the yard owner where to take his hardware business and slammed down the phone. Jack sat across the room, seething at his desk, chewing his stubby cigar to shreds in anguish. Finally, he exploded at his son-in-law, ripping into him with the furor of months of pent-up frustration.

Jack was outraged at Frank's cavalier treatment of customers. He called him a two-bit punk, a snotnose leech, and a dumb sonofabitch. Then as if his father's salvo was a declaration of open season on Frank, Michael now waded into his brother-in-law at every turn. He'd blast Frank for insignificant typographical errors in bid sheets. He reamed him out on the shipping floor for one or two case undercounts on lines of 50 cases, six deep. His father's sufferance was clearly implied, and Michael wasted no words.

Frank had come to feel at home in $250 suits. He began coming home nights wretchedly heartsick. Anger was a new emotion to him. He let it out at Jennifer with an unabated fury that frightened their two small children.

Jennifer once again called her father. She demanded to know why he and Michael were ganging up on Frank. Again intimidated by his baby's threats, Jack promptly eased off Frank and suggested that Michael do the same for the sake of Jenny's marriage. So now the success or failure of Jenny's marriage had insidiously become a liability on the balance sheet of R. & J. Cates & Sons.

A quiet period of about five months followed, after which Frank began asserting himself again. Now, after nearly 3 years of working in the company, he suddenly sensed a simple fact which nothing in the world could change: Michael and Jenny were equal heirs to the Cates estate; Michael's majority position was held as a result of a voting trust arrangement. The idea was for Jack's children to own the business half and half, but for Michael to have management control. Learning this spurred Frank forward. He now assumed the role of caretaker and surrogate for his wife's interests. He convinced Jenny to ask her father about this fact. She did and, to her surprise, learned that her father and brother had considered themselves guardians of her rights. She now advised them both that her husband would speak for her. She urged Frank on to more audacious action, pressing him to prove his mettle against his hard-driving brother-in-law and noisome sister-in-law.

Frank now got his head. He reorganized the entire inner management system of the company, replacing old, skilled order takers with younger people working a new WATS telephone system. The results were predictably absymal as one would expect they would be with any sudden new shock to an old system. Frank pushed on. He computerized the whole warehousing system and, once more, the results were disastrous. Overhead soared, problems mounted, but Frank stubbornly clung to his task and kept rolling ahead. Jack and Michael were so deeply engaged in massive industrial contracting, dashing back and forth during complex negotiations, that they abandoned the daily running of the business to Frank.

Finally, Frank's force feeding of the company began showing results. The internal organization was exemplary, efficient, and forged together in a tight network of loyalties around Frank. He was working every night till 10, Saturdays, Sundays, pouring out the sweat in buckets. And he did not let anyone forget it.

After a time, he merely took as much salary as he wanted without a murmur from either his brother-in-law or father-in-law.

Jenny found a house in a newer, more chic suburb north of the city and furnished it like Versailles. At last, after so many years of being number two, she pulled up alongside her sister-in-law; the last inch of the status gap closed.

This jolted Susan Bellows Cates. She'd spent the past five years harmlessly occupied with spending colossal sums of money on her lavish home, her children, and herself. The final upward thrust of her brother-in-law and sister-in-law into a social status compatable with her own jarred her into action. She felt compelled to butt into company affairs to protect the interests of her husband and father-in-law who'd built the Cates Company into a gold mine. She would not let that golden goose be cooked by Frank Talbot. She pleaded the upper-middle class, bored housewife syndrome to Michael. She'd tried everything she said. Encounter groups, sensitivity training, pottery workshops, gardening classes—all of it left her empty. It was only in the real tough world of business where a woman could feel alive again. Too busy and too exhausted to debate the point, Michael gave in and arranged for Susan to "come in Tuesdays and Thursdays" to help out around the office. Now the battle was joined.

Frank was asked to find meaningful work for Susan. What was he to do with her? She possessed no office skills. He tried to make her useful, assigning her filing, order taking, telephoning for lunch, and envelope typing.

She pouted to Michael during the drive home each Tuesday and Thursday. She charged that Frank was vindictively assigning her to moron's work. Michael wisely replied that if she wanted interesting work, she should look for a job elsewhere.

Susan took the offensive. She accused Frank of covering up the errors of half the office because he had hired them. She charged him with flirting with "every little telephone operator" and "growling at customers." Michael initially shrugged off these accusations, but Susan persisted and finally won her husband's weary ear. He was inclined to want to believe bad stories about his brother-in-law because Frank had become an equal force in the company. Michael relented. He allowed Susan to begin spying on Frank.

She maintained copious notes of Frank's actions and re-

ported them in detail to her husband each night. This kind of
lunacy simply couldn't continue unnoticed. One day, one of
Frank's closest assistants found Susan's diary beneath a sheaf of
papers. Not wishing to alarm Frank, the man, who was also an old
friend of Jenny's, reported the contents to her. An enraged Jenny
confronted her father with Xeroxed copies of Susan's spy pages.
Jack then confronted Michael with the notes. Michael froze in
surly silence, offended by his father's accusing tone. Within a
week, Michael and his father were not on speaking terms. Neither
man spoke to Frank. Jennifer and Susan publicly traded insults
at local beauty parlors. Both daughter and daughter-in-law were
barred from the office. The three men began conducting business by memo. It was an ugly scene.

The atmosphere became so charged with mutual suspicion
that, against his better judgement, Jack was forced to yield to
Michael's suggestion that they separate the sales and service departments and establish a downtown sales office where Michael
could work in peace.

Michael would move out with the sales force and Frank
would remain at the warehouse and service center at the old
location. The new downtown offices cost nearly $25,000 to fur-
nish (the decorator's touch being added by Susan Cates) and
$2,000 a month to run. It was an idiotic waste and evidence of
the corrosive effects of family bickering in small businesses. No
significant business was transacted in the downtown office. Michael was away most of the time. When he came into the gor-
geous penthouse, he passed the time toying with the affections
of a beautifully upholstered receptionist, sipping Scotch sours,
and conjecturing about what his brother-in-law was plotting back
at headquarters.

Michael couldn't stand the tension. He now took level aim
at Frank. He met with his father and insisted that the whole office
be moved downtown and that only a stockroom and warehouse
remain at the old location. Frank cried foul. He had been quietly
negotiating on his own with the county industrial development
commissioners for a new home for the whole company in an
industrial park twenty miles out of town. He was close to comp-
leting a deal that would give Cates all the room in the world to
expand with virtually no capital investment, with an attractive tax

abatement package, and an option to buy a new building. Everyone at Cates had dreamed about just such a program, including Michael. But now the son of the son of the great Randolph Cates was more obdurate than ever. He was determined to escalate this family folly into a duel to the death.

Urged on by their wives like knights at a medieval tournament, Michael Cates and Frank Talbot raised lances and thundered toward each other for a final, bloody showdown.

Little insulting memos about the move to the industrial park versus the move downtown were exchanged daily. Frank began sending pollution and air quality reports clipped from the daily newspaper to Michael. Michael replied with advertisements for hamster farms. They soon dropped the gentlemanly pose of memos and went at each other face to face, locked in mortal combat. Pushing and shoving matches grew closer and closer. Michael's hot temper was well known as was his large collection of firearms. Frank privately confessed to his wife one evening after waking up at 4 A.M. in a sweat, "I dreamed your brother shot me." Paranoia spread unabated. Frank bought a .45 pistol and hid it in a locked drawer of his desk. He was ready for anything.

The vicious hatreds penetrated every minute of the working day. Jack Cates watched helplessly. One day Jack needed some information and walked over to Frank's desk and tried the drawer he knew it would be in. It was jammed. He jimmied it open and found the .45 lying there. He was stunned. When Frank returned from lunch, Jack threw the gun on his desk. A shaking Frank confessed his fears. "Michael told some of the guys at the club he was going to kill me."

"Michael . . . Michael, kill . . . kill you? What have I done here? What have I done?" Jack cried out, bursting into hysterical tears. He was stupified; yet, he could not deny having seen the deterioration over the past year. He had to act.

The following day, Jack Cates called a meeting which included the company lawyer, the company banker, Michael, and Frank.

"We're going to decide, here today, which way we go. It's either out to Oakwood Park, or straight downtown," Jack began, his voice cracking. Frank was asked to present his case first. He did and did it well. Michael followed with an equally eloquent plea for a broader scope downtown. Though blood was thicker than water (and always is, *always*), Frank's argument was stronger and Michael's petulance showed through his presentation. Jack and his advisers agreed to Frank's plan.

Now that Michael's ears were pinned back, it came the turn of Frank. Jack stood up and paced toward the window. Then, slowly turning, he said, "Now that this moving business is decided, I'm getting out. I'm announcing my retirement. I'm handing my chair over to you, Michael."

Michael, stunned by the blow minutes before, recovered quickly and dashed over to embrace his father. He turned and ran from the room to call Susan, halting momentarily to sneer at a chastened Frank. This was not what his father had hoped for. His decision had not sobered either of the two young men. The forces of bitterness had been unleashed and now played out their final iniquities.

Hearing about her brother's promotion to the company presidency, Jenny turned cold and bitchy. She would answer no calls from either her mother or father. She barred them from the house and refused to let them see her children. She was humiliated. The very thought that her own father would create an atmosphere in which Michael and his harridan wife could abuse her husband was beyond her comprehension.

Jenny had a short memory. She'd conveniently forgotten that until she and Susan began sticking their noses into the business in a competitive battle for status, she would probably have met the news of her brother's promotion with great joy. She'd forgotten that in the past she really loved her brother. She couldn't understand the forces she herself had unleashed. She joined her parents in a deepening depression.

Susan now sought sweet revenge on Frank. She nagged Michael to break him. But Michael, finally spent from the battle, staggered around town in drunken confusion. Why, he asked, had he brought such despair down around the shoulders of his little sister? Why was everyone so miserable? He told Susan he didn't care if Frank installed a ten-foot marble statue of himself in the middle of the warehouse. All his energies, normally diverted toward healthy business pursuits, had been dissipated in ridiculous debate, raging resentments, and flaming filial passions. He was a spent young man. His appetite for battle was sated.

Frank was charged with directing the move to the new Oakwood Park facility. He was similarly embittered and disillusioned. He had won, but he had lost. Not that he'd ever expected to become head of the company. But he resented the quid pro quo manner in which his father-in-law approved his plan, then gratuitously slapped his face by announcing Michael's promotion on its heels. He sensed a vengeful impulse in Jack to remind him that blood was indeed, thicker than water, and that offended his gentlemanly sensibilities and stripped him of dignity.

These results were the farthest things from Jack's mind. He had hoped to reconcile the boys and to show by example what it was to be chastened for a greater good. It was a lousy morality lesson as things turned out.

This disillusionment hardened into corporate inertia. Managers who sought out Michael for crucial decisions were brusquely told to see Frank. Frank was out playing golf. Michael was playing tennis. Neither cared anymore, and the figures soon bore out this neglect. Contract bids went unanswered; competitors were not met; stores were not serviced; salesmen went their own way without direction or purpose. The new facility badly needed a strong hand to guide it. Instead, it floundered in indifference. The shining new building was a testimony to the achievements of the Cates Company, and its confused inside a testimony to its folly.

Conditions deteriorated so rapidly that Jack Cates was forced out of retirement in an attempt to reconcile the brothers-in-law. They met in the lakeside hunting lodge, exchanged empty pleasantries, and pledged "better cooperation." This statement was about as revealing of progress as the diplomatic "frank and cordial exchange of views" jargon. The two young men, having depleted their energies emotionally murdering each other, had no strength left for the more wholesome battle of restoring their business to health. Convinced he could no longer count on either man, Jack sought out an executive recruiting firm and hurriedly brought in a team of three new "department head coordinators."

These three new men, led by Jack, valiantly attempted the rescue. But things had deteriorated badly. Jack spent half his days conferring between Frank and Michael, rummaging through contracts, trying to puzzle out policy. Michael sank into an increasing enervation of spirit. He flew off to safaris in Africa for months at a time. Frank began speculating wildly in the commodities market. Jack reviewed the year-end figures. There was no way the company could last through the new year without massive surgery. Jack was tired too. He called a close friend and competitor and sold out the business for less than 60¢ on the dollar. His accountant later advanced the opinion that Jack made a good deal. He was, the man figured, about four months away from bankruptcy at the time.

Michael and Frank weren't even there for the closing. Michael was in Sardinia, and Frank had flown to Chicago to talk over a soybean deal.

AUTOPSY

The death of a business like R. & J. Cates & Sons because of familial conflict is not merely tragic. It's criminal. How did Jack's paternal love bring about the very processes which were to drag his business and family down?

1] Jack allowed his daughter to propose a solution to her own money problems which affected the family business.

2] Jack subjected his son to the terrible pressures of a contemporary in the family competing for psychological primacy. It did not matter that Michael was the unchallenged heir apparent. Frank's entry diluted the feeling that he was and fostered the notion that should Michael ever falter, Frank was not far behind. These are normally mere ripples in a large business, but in a small one, they are swift and treacherous undercurrents.

3] Jack made Frank a vassal to his son. Although Michael hesitated to pull rank on his brother-in-law, at times, it was needed and necessary. Michael could not, however, bring himself around to chew out Frank in front of "the help." So instead of ventilating normal business tensions in a healthy way, resentments festered. Michael unwisely dumped the chore of correcting Frank's presumptions upon his father who was, in turn, under pressure to lay off from his daughter.

4] Jack permitted the business to be used as a weapon to satisfy his daughter-in-law's voracious appetite for status. His daughter-in-law's uses of wealth wrenched his sensibilities, but that was not the issue. He'd made no contract with Susan Cates, and if her husband was similarly offended, he'd have stopped her. But he didn't. Susan and Michael loved each other. He wanted her to have everything. She was hardly a criminal for venting her healthy desires. She was no hypocrite. Jack saw this. He refused to step in between them to impose his will. He correctly assumed it was none of his affair. Yet it was Susan's wild spending that threw Jennifer into the poor Little Match Girl pose.

5] Jack seduced Frank by dependency. There's plenty of room for healthy sniping among in-laws. When financial dependency in the form of a cushy life style enters the picture, things drastically change. There's no safety value anymore. Frank hesitated to contend with his father-in-law lest he be toppled back into the little accounting firm. So Frank kept his own frustrations bottled up inside until he could let it all out on someone who couldn't fight back. That someone was, of course, Jenny, his wife, whose happiness was, after all, the ostensible objective of the whole exercise to begin with.

Randolph Cates had dissolved a profitable business rather than subject it to the psychopressure cooker that he felt the elevation of one of his four sons to heir apparent would create. The symbolism of this act was apparently lost on Jack Cates.

He brought Frank in, basically, to assure that his

daughter's financial status would be equal to his son's. He felt that Frank's presence legitimatized the dispensation of largess because a straightforward and probably more honest subsidy offended his Puritan mentality. In this way, he felt he could indulge the daughter he loved without depriving the son he loved in a way that suited his own ethics.

Whose fault was it that Jack couldn't see that all he needed do was see that his daughter received a fat dividend every year equal to that of the bonus monies drawn by his son?

Family businesses can be successful. I know one sensibly run business which has been thriving for nearly fifty years. Father, son, and son-in-law draw equal salaries, dividends, and bonuses. The father has designated the son as the heir apparent publicly. There can be no bitching because everyone gets the same. Certainly, the two younger men can sit around grumbling in private about who *deserves* more, but all he need do is bitch aloud and the father will simply advise the bitcher to *take more*, with the clear understanding that for every extra dollar he takes, his contemporary has the right to take one too. So at the end of each fiscal year, the three men sit down and decide to either vote or not vote themselves more money. And that is the end of it. Differences in their lives are purely a matter of style and taste, not substance.

The central force in this working system is the strong father figure. He is the court of last appeal. More important, there are no illusions. The succession has been firmly established. The men operate under that working knowledge and conflict is *controlled*. But too many families contain abrasive sons-in-law, or viciously acquisitive daughters, or daughters-in-law, or meddling parents. When these totally untenable personalities appear, it would seem wise to go the way of a straight-off subsidy, or even payoff if you will, to the offensive party. It may revolt you to pay off anyone, but one thing is certain, you won't be one-tenth as revolted as when you wake up one morning and find yourself hovering on the edge of bankruptcy.

The failure of family businesses in conflict are mostly failures of the heart or spirit. Like it or not, you are your brother-in-law's keeper. So you might as well call him up now, invite him over for a drink, look into his beady eyes, and say, "I bet you thought I resented you when you came into the business, old buddy . . ."

2

The Prophet and the Promised Land

> "If there arise in the midst of thee a prophet, or a dreamer of dreams . . . saying: Let us go after other gods, which thou has not known . . . thou shalt not hearken unto the words of that prophet . . ."
>
> —Deuteronomy 13:2

S E V E R A L years ago, I sat watching an old college friend moaning in pain as he ran his pudgy finger across columns of sales figures of his company's previous month.

"Fifth goddamn month of decline," he volunteered in disgust. "I've just got to get my men off their fat asses." As Steve wheeled his own 250-pound frame around in his red, plush leather chair, he continued his plaintive refrain.

"I've got to get some new blood going here. We're dead on our asses. We need a freakin' blood transfusion. A real guy, you know, someone to come in here and get all my lazy sonsofbitches working again, selling again. They're just spoiled. And they need someone to whip 'em." Without awaiting a reply, he shifted to some personal matter and invited me to lunch. He ate his way through a gargantuan Italian feast downed with two bottles of red wine. He leaned back and stared at the restaurant ceiling, puffing a long, thin cigar.

"I don't want any guy with a long résumé. I'm willing to pay. I want a real hotshot operator. What are these sales VP's going for these days?" he asked vacantly.

I replied, confessing my total ignorance of the executive personnel field or prevailing wage scales. But one thing was now certain. It seemed to me that my friend's problems were only beginning.

I offered some free advice. I urged him to subject his whole business to one quiet weekend of thoughtful, quiet, reflection, away from his wife and children and away from dinner table marathons. Perhaps his product line was weak. Maybe the sales force morale was low because of something not readily apparent. Was he delivering goods on time? Was his plant turning out shoddy stuff? What were his competitors doing?

"That, old friend," he said blowing a perfect smoke ring, "is a lot of that marketing crap we learned in school. I don't need to reflect in a pool or contemplate my belly. What I need is a good old-fashioned barn burning Sales VP to get my sales organization in shape. It's just overweight."

I cracked a sardonic smile. The irony of his comment had apparently evaded him. That bothered me more than anything he said. It meant he was beginning to live in his own world. And his world was one where men sought prophets and Messiahs because the truth was too messy.

Unfortunately, Steve's business is dead and buried now. Its lying there among the rubble of his stubborn misconceptions about the capacity of prophets to see, of Messiahs to save, and, mostly, of new brooms to sweep clean.

Steve's love of heroism went all the way back to his college days. He was unquestionably the fastest-moving, hardest-driving man in our graduating class. He was chairman of this, president of that, everyone's choice for "most popular and most likely to succeed." Class hero. There was no doubt that, in 10 years, Steve Baker would be the richest guy in the world.

His future successes in business were to lead him to believe in his own Messianic powers and, eventually, to seek a Messiah when he needed help.

In every position he held after college, he was heralded as a savior; he was aggressive and resourceful; and his bosses, whose businesses boomed after his arrival, were duly impressed. Within a few years, he was outearning, outworking, and outscrewing every one of his contemporaries. But Steve began to itch. No matter how much he earned, his bosses always earned more. What Steve needed now was his own business where every check that arrived every day had a piece with his name written on it.

It was while Steve was looking around for a business that he met Underwriter Hayes, a man whose record made him something of a genius. Steve was seduced by Hayes' brilliance and listened harder to him than anyone else.

Underwriter Hayes, it seemed, had this little gem of a com-

pany which was floundering for want of the strong leadership
only Steve could provide. The company's net worth was easily
$1,000,000 in tangible assets but, because of Underwriter Hayes'
firm's pivitol position in the company's stock, he could arrange
for Steve to buy into a majority position for under $300,000 in
cash and he would arrange financing for an additional $400,000
in notes. "Its just seventy cents on the dollar for net worth,"
Hayes said, "and they're making money. But the family must get
out. The father had a stroke."

The company, Sunnyboy Specialities, Inc., manufactured
and distributed advertising specialities such as ball-point pens
shaped like baseball bats, desk sets, calendars, stationery, plastic
graphs, and measuring devices that had special imprints like,
"This slide rule is a handy reminder to slide down to Big Jimmy's
Auto Collision & Fender Co. 456-7800 Next Time You Crash or
Smash"

Sunnyboy Specialities, Inc. was the largest company of its
kind, doing over $9,000,000 a year at its height in 1962. When
Steve looked over the figures, he saw this had sunk to under
$5,000,000. Yet, because of a continuing low operating cost and
decent profit margins, the company managed to remain sound,
with over $500,000 in cash and receivables and $500,000 in machinery, plant, etc.

The time had come, Hayes said, for Steve to make the big
move. He was too smart a guy not to own his own company.
Flattered by the attentions of someone he respected, Steve bit.
Hayes could say no wrong or do no wrong. Yet, there was something else that drew Steve into this new venture. Steve felt he
could move the company out of the premium field and into the
consumer field with products manufactured in the same plant. He
sensed a big-time smell about Sunnyboy. Against the chorus of
boos from his business friends, Steve saw a star shining over the
horizon and three wise men on camels coming toward his office.
His friends wisely warned Steve that Underwriter Hayes was just
looking for a sucker to take over another one of his fizzled public
stock issues. Steve resented their character portrait of Hayes,
admonishing them to watch their mouths and clucking his tongue
about how some guys will never understand big business. So
Steve took over Sunnyboy Specialities and became a member of

Underwriter Hayes' athletic club at the same time. His first official act was to rename the company Sunshine Industries, Inc., with a pretentious logo designed by a properly pretentious expensive design firm recommended by Hayes. The new slogan, "WE make the world a happier place," was appropriate to the state of mind of Underwriter Hayes when Steve forked over the money for the company. But the slogan took a deadly turn for Steve, as the following year was to show.

Steve's arrival at Sunshine Industries was heralded by the employees as a Messianic blessing. That kind of approval fit Steve. His weaknesses for Messiahs either in the form of himself or others was to be tested soon.

The factory employees, having been advised that the arcane, stodgy, miserly, old management was being replaced by an enlightened and generous young management, promptly threatened to strike if long-neglected wage demands were not instantly met. The Sunshine workers had apparently learned well from New York City's Transit Workers Union, who similarly took, on face value, the press and campaign rhetoric of John V. Lindsay in 1965 and struck the subways the week Lindsay took office. It was then up to Lindsay to prove how expansive an outlook he had as against Mayor Wagner whom he had characterized as "tired." The Sunshine workers now tested Steve's spirit.

He was not found wanting. With piles of unshipped orders menacing him, he panicked into a blackmail settlement with the workers lest his well-publicized takeover of Sunshine besmirch his carefully polished public image. We don't seek to suggest here that either the subway workers or the Sunshine workers were overpaid plutocrats undeserving of a sensible increase. Quite the contrary, both were probably grossly underpaid. But what we do suggest is this: He who claims to be enlightened in business should be prepared that others will take him at his word. Corporate intelligence, enlightenment, are worthy objectives, perhaps the worthiest of all in our increasingly finite planet. But they have a price.

The punishing settlement shot Steve's labor costs up over 15% over 3 years. Worse still, the plant settlement triggered long-dormant unrest in the office and Steve was soon besieged with requests from department heads for salary increases for long-time employees. Steve was again forced to capitulate, thus laying another heavy stone around his neck. The wildcat strike lasted 10 days.

During this time, a critical new product introduction was delayed, throwing askew a carefully laid marketing plan. Steve now gained control and personally directed the relaunch. It succeeded. It went so well in fact that original sales projections for the new digital calendar were exceeded by 25%. Competition, however, as is its birthright, copied the product and entered with a cheaper price. Steve was caught with a long inventory position on the item and began dealing it down to head off competition. It was to little avail. For some reason, he could not get the company mechanism to respond to his will. Frustrated, against the wall and growing bitter, Steve began eating obsessively—stuffing himself at every opportunity and looking around for someone to blame.

A man with a compulsion to pin blame is equally wont to seek Messiahs. It was at this time that the thought of a savior entered Steve's mind. That's when we had our chat. Dismissing me and many other friends who counseled otherwise, Steve now decided that what his drowning enterprise needed was a big, strapping, sun-tanned lifeguard.

He arrived in the person of Ralph Oaks, 45, 6-feet 4, with a resume which read like one long citation of a war hero some small-district Representative would read into the Congressional Record. Letters of recommendation from heads of *Fortune* 500 Companies reached flights of Churchillian oratory. As Sales VP of the small-appliance division of a corporate behemoth, he'd earned $50,000 a year. He wanted $65,000 to quit his job, plus stock and all the perquisites of his station.

In fairness to Steve, it should be noted here that Ralph looked like General Patton and exuded that same rugged sense of command that George C. Scott so intelligently brought to the screen in that role. It was precisely this quality that Steve sought and bought. He felt importuned, attacked, and begirded by foe, and in such a situation, a guy needs a general.

The easiest sale in the world is, of course, to sell a salesman. It took one interview for Ralph to sell Steve. "There is nothing," Ralph had said during the meeting, "that cannot be cured in any sales organization by the simple rumor that the new guy is a sonofabitch. We're gonna make them think I'm the biggest bastard who ever walked this earth. Then you just watch the action." Ralph was beginning to sound more like Jesus Christ every minute. He was hired.

Ralph's first act in "office" was to undertake a long road trip to "kiss some asses, goose some asses, burn some asses, and kick some asses clear out of the company." Ralph's anal notions about stimulating sales also included pinching some asses, an incurable habit he'd picked up in the service and which soon cost him his secretary.

So with 1,300 bucks a week and a Diner's Card to nourish him, Ralph hit the road. Chicago, Dallas, San Francisco, St. Louis, Atlanta, Boston, Baltimore—a string of cities serviced by some of Sunshine's oldest and most permanently anchored sales representatives. Ralph mailed daily reports to Steve. They spoke over the phone twice a week. A month after Ralph was out, Steve called me.

"Do you know what Ralph did?" he asked in apparent relish.

"Tell me" I replied, awaiting an I told-you-so-you-dumb-bastard type of a story.

"Ralph stole a mother of an order away from Acme. He kicked out our old rep in Chicago and put on a new one who bangs the premium buyer of one of the biggest accounts we never sold and the new guy writes a $50,000 order the first week with this chick."

"Looks like you made one helluva good choice," I said, unconvinced.

"Sure did, you old dumb bastard," he said laughing. I then politely refused his offer of a good lunch. I was on a mild diet trying to shed 5 pounds. I sat at my desk munching cottage cheese from a plastic tub. Was it beginning to taste like humble pie?

Ralph Oaks returned in triumph from the front lines. In hand, over $100,000 worth of new business; in attache case, $5,600 in accumulated tabs. Ralph and Steve sat together in Steve's office discussing the overall outlook seen after a month-long road trip.

Ralph began with a lucidly crisp description of the state of the Sunshine sales organization. Ralph's credibility was unimpeachable, the $100,000 in new orders had seen to that. But Steve also wanted badly to believe, to cling to every word, to heed the Messiah's pronouncements. Ralph analyzed and grouped the whole mess into five basic problems. After ticking off each major problem area, he admonished his boss, "Steve, if we can get this thing on track, we'll have a record quarter." Steve nervously nodded agreement as he shoved another dollop of Baskin Robbins' Rocky Road into his grinning mouth.

What specifics did Ralph's strategic diagnosis contain? How did he go about solving the problems? Here are the problems as Ralph saw them, the remedies he used and the results.

PROBLEM: Fat and lazy sales representatives.

The company's commission reps had grown fat and lazy. They carried too many conflicting lines and didn't devote enough time to the Sunshine lines. They didn't make enough sales calls, didn't follow up leads from the home office because they were getting too rich on reorders from old accounts that came in automatically. Ralph strengthened his case by describing in detail the life style of one Sunshine rep whose sales were off.

The man, it seemed, lived in a massive Tudor house on 3 acres in a plush midwestern suburb. He retained three household servants, one of whom spent a day a week polishing the $30,000 Mercedes 600 sedan. "This bum hasn't been out on the territory for months. No customer ever sees the guy. He's got a telephone business. Sits there like Henry the Eighth, eating fruit and collecting commissions for doing nothing." Steve listened with an intense, deliciously vengeful anger when Ralph told him the story. "I didn't even call you. I fired the sonofabitch on the spot, right there in his own house, while his goddamn butler was mixing me a Scotch." Steve was at the point of orgasm as Ralph drove into his peroration. "What we need out there are hungry tigers, guys who want to sweat their balls off for a buck, not these fucking dukes who want to live like semi-retired Khans."

SOLUTION: Throw the sonsobitches out.

The company should dump the over-fat sales representatives in the lucrative territories and replace them with house salesmen. This would reduce selling costs and dramatically increase the number of sales calls.

Ralph immediately discharged five of the most prosperous, fat, and lazy sales representatives in American business history. They were rapidly replaced with youthful, salaried "pros." The territories into which this hypo was shot had yielded annual sales of Sunshine products of around $1,000,000 for 5 years. Six months after the adminstration of this quick cure, sales were under $150,00, heading for an annual $300,000 at best, or 70% under the fat and lazy era. Why did Ralph's sensible solution (or so it appeared) misfire?

Upon being relieved of the representation rights to the Sunshine line, all five lazy, fat-assed reps suddenly got ambitious. They dug up cheaper competing lines. This was to be naturally anticipated. But the switch was made so fast that Sunshine's new men were unprepared to fight on two fronts. On one front—the attack from below—the traditional cheaper imports and strictly shlock price lines; from the flank, Sunshine's former reps lavishing the territory shamelessly with graft, trips, good times, booze, broads, and "introductory specials" on their new lines financed by their own funds. The old lazy guys were using monies earned from Steve's company to whip the daylights out of Steve's fiery new men.

The former sales representatives had admittedly been ripping off Sunshine. Ralph's analysis was correct and pointed; replacing the representatives with fewer salaried men was honestly a good idea. However, Ralph's fatal error was in timing. The former representatives, in many cases, had been servicing the same customers over 25 years, developing cozy relationships. In a highly duplicable field such as Sunshine was in, this should have thrown up an immediate red flag in Steve's mind. He should have remembered his own experience back in his sales days. He should have recalled how he stripped his old employer clean within 2 years, based primarily on the uniqueness of his relationships with his customers. A salesman may be paid by the house but his natural inclination is to see the customer, not the house, as his life line. He can always duplicate the house. Cultivating customers is a tedious process, requiring patience and restraint that only time can provide.

The former reps had complained too. They were demoralized, they reported, by management's notable lack of creativity and new product development. Why were they always blamed for sinking sales? Why didn't management come up with the lines that would increase sales? They'd grouse, but they wouldn't scream because they, too, didn't wish to rock the boat. They could, indeed, spend the day on the phone taking simple reorders and from that make substantial commissions.

Who had there been to listen anyway? In the previous 3 years, the former owners, had sat counting the minutes until Underwriter Hayes could find a turkey to buy them out. They weren't moving on new products, nor were they inclined to listen. Such a situation can't be written on a financial statement, and Underwriter Hayes had been less than candid. But caveat emptor. Steve should have known better. As for Ralph, he'd fingered the symptom, not the disease. So its ravaging effects on Sunshine sales continued. Ralph's "big change in the territory" was a disaster.

PROBLEM: The line was overpriced.

The Sunshine line wasn't competitive. Ralph had compared all of Sunshine's volume lines to those of its two principal competitors, and item for item, in nearly every case, Sunshine's prices were at least 15% higher. Steve mildly rejoined that he was aware of that but that the simple truth was that Sunshine's products were better and cost more to produce. Ralph reminded Steve that companies buying mass premium merchandise didn't buy quality but price. And it was time Sunshine faced it.

SOLUTION: Lower the prices.

Deal the line heavy, forget quality, substitute "adequate" materials, regain lost customers, and, finally, "when all the business is back in our tent, we slowly raise the prices—so slowly the bastards won't be aware of what we're doing. We finish by getting more dough because we have the quality name, for the same shit the competition now gets a low-ball price for." As an eminently successful and terribly shrewd salesman himself, Steve saw the strategic skill in what Ralph recommended. But somewhere he suspected a flaw in the logic. He didn't, however, give it any more thought at the moment. He was too entranced by Ralph's relentless military manner.

Ralph demanded a cost analysis, product by product. He learned that the company could withstand some heavy trade promotion, but only over a brief period. Trade promotions chronically overrun themselves. The Sunshine men had been trained never to demand price promotions except the two a year the former owners ran by rote. Consequently, they didn't expect anything. A price was a price. You took it or left it. And this is why the Sunshine commission men had interwoven themselves so tightly with their customers. They often paid off in personal favors and swag to get Sunshine business which would have ordinarily been shut out by overpricing. The former management knew this too well but artfully looked the other way. If these men wished to pay off, it was their money and their business, and when willing old Steve came in led by Hayes, panting, the slick old pair weren't about to tell him how much of their business had been bought.

Ralph had learned about this on the road, but he preferred to let it go unheeded because it did not serve either his personal ambition, or Steve's proclivity to believe he was being totally ill-served by these men. He listened instead to other representatives who complained about pricing policies. He should have known better. There isn't a salesman in the world who ever thinks his company's price is right. There can't be. After all, it's the salesman, on the line of fire, who bears the brunt of competitive attacks.

So when big old General Ralph Oaks flies into the territory one evening, sits you down over a stiff drink, places his hand on your shoulder and says, "Open up, old buddy. C'mon guy, spill it, I'm just a peddler like you. What do we need to get this old turkey back on its feet?" What does Jones the salesman say?

"They're knocking the living shit out of us on price." He

shows the big-time N.Y. VP General item by item how stupid the company's prices are. Having heard this fraudulent litany over 20 years, our General nods in willing agreement.

Ralph's motives were genuine. Yet again, it was a symptom and not the central malfunction that would be treated by lowered prices. He started cutting prices, fully cognizant that the minute his promotion expired, he'd lose the price customers back to the competitor with the cheapest price on the street. Why shouldn't a man running a business have as much sense when he shops as a housewife does when she shops the specials each week at a different supermarket? "Goddamned whores," Ralph muttered when his promotional aftermath produced no new regular price business. That was unfair. Customers buy for their own weal, not for Ralph Oaks. Still spurred by his conviction that a price war was a battle to the end, Ralph revived the promotion, knowing Sunshine could not bear such a fierce and sustained attack on its profit margins during a time of rising overheads. He was a medieval physician applying leeches to his king, confident he was easing his pain, where, in many cases, he was bleeding him to death.

Salesmen rightfully should scream like banshees when any vital aspect of selling or marketing comes to their attention. Ralph didn't need the old-school bitching about prices only. He had to know about product, about who was being paid off, about where and when a price special to a particular customer might pay dividends. Even then, he shouldn't have depended on his dog-faces in the trenches. He should have known it himself. Sales dragged.

PROBLEM: The home office was bad news

The New York sales office was woefully below the task of backing up the men in the field. Samples arrived late or not at all, price quotations took weeks, inventory data was sporadic, new product introductions were aborted by out-of-stock problems.

SOLUTION: Fire the stupid sonsobitches.

Clean up the Sales Service Department. Convert it into a Marketing Services Department. Hire a "heavyweight" to run it, "so the boys on the front line will feel Command Headquarters is right behind them."

Ralph was given total control by Steve. His sense of command awed Steve. He could do no wrong. What was now happening was "the crunch." Steve was admonished to "see it through."

Ralph fired ten people in the sales service and order departments. Most of those fired were low-level managers and clerks. Of the ten he dismissed, nine justly deserved to be fired. But Ralph's failure as the Messiah of the office was not because he fired one person who didn't deserve it, but because he didn't fire the one person who did deserve it, more than anyone else. His failure as a judge of manpower was fatal here.

Fred Healy, Sales Services Manager, was the critical link between the field and the office. He worked long hours—sweating over distribution of paper work and reports. Ralph liked that kind of "staff work." It's easy to fire an obvious goof-off or dummy. It's not so easy to see through a Fred. Struggling each day, "holding up the whole sales department home base," he was, in fact, standing as the singularly prime impediment to the efficient functioning of the support departments.

As the crossroads cop of the sales department, Fred was misdirecting everyone. He issued wrong directions to the sample department. He simply couldn't cope with pressure and, when rushed, he blundered into stupid errors.

So after a time, he unconsciously shifted his concept of his job from that of a traffic cop to that of a P.R. man. He spent more time exchanging jokes with the representatives who called in than exchanging information. He saw his job as a morale booster, a brother-at-the-home-office crony job rather than as a vital communications link with the field. In his cozy, low-pressure way, Fred survived the blood bath. In its wake, Ralph hired ten new people. They were all excellent finds. But all shared one fatal disability. They all had to learn from Fred.

In a matter of months, he had ten clear-thinking, reasonably efficient people in an utter state of confusion. They could not break through the veritable maze of cross-references and tortuously intricate idiocies Fred had built into the department. The result of Ralph's program to improve headquarters back-up backfired. No significant improvement was produced. Order processing was as sluggish as ever. The bottlenecks remained unbroken. The people around Fred had been the symptom, but Fred was the disease.

PROBLEM: Mail order division ran its own show.

The Sunshine mail order division was operated by a skilled company veteran named Daniel Dean. His operation produced nearly 30% of all sales and over 50% of profits. Mail order carried the heaviest profit contribution to the corporate statement. Dean was no fool. Instead of pointing out this weakness to previous management, he had permitted the company's dependence on his division to deepen. (Where have we heard this before?) He knew the previous owners were dying to sell out, and when they did, he'd always have a sound case for himself with the new ownership. And that's exactly the way it happened. When Steve bought the company, his first intelligent impulse was to let the guy alone. As a result, Dean had priority and command over the loyalties of the office staff. His work got done first and often only his work got done at all. Ralph's hunger for power could not tolerate Daniel's formidable command position.

SOLUTION: Make mail order responsible to sales.

Ralph decided that mail order should be placed under his direction because it was a sales activity. Steve meekly agreed but privately wondered about a clash between Dean and the new man. If fealty was what Ralph thought was needed, however, Daniel would have to bend. Survival was at stake.

Ralph quickly established a pleasant working relationship with Daniel by explaining in honest, precise language the reasons why his division had to be brought into his constellation. Corporate survival was at stake and, if Daniel pledged his cooperation, he (Ralph) would not meddle in Daniel's daily operations. Daniel somewhat suspiciously agreed.

Ralph had intelligently handled Daniel, but he could not

restrain his own need for power too long; he soon began to lean on Daniel. He wrote a memo to Daniel the following week, requesting him to report more frequently on progress and sales and asking for forecasts of mail business. Daniel bit hard at this memo, but willing to cooperate with Ralph to preserve his fat salary, he gritted his teeth and complied.

Daniel prepared trenchant, well-documented reports each month, packed with important figures and a variety of recommendations on many vital issues and policies. Ralph received Daniel's reports, had his secretary stamp them "Received" with the time and date and shoved them into his briefcase for "weekend reading." Only on weekends, Ralph was either busy cavorting at his club or cavorting on the road. He never read one.

One important report, in which Daniel strongly recommended conversion of the entire advertising speciality line to mail and building a new consumer products group from scratch (as Steve had originally intended), was carried by Ralph in his case for months unread until it was lost. Adoption of Daniel's plan may have sharply reduced selling costs and placed Sunshine into the consumer field at a small level of investment. Ralph had never even glanced at it, so Steve only heard about it from Daniel in casual conversation. And Steve had become so hopelessly absorbed in battling machine breakdowns, raw materials supplies, labor and legal woes, and worsening financial troubles that he had little time to listen to the babblings of Daniel. Ralph's hit-and-run advice became policy in hours. Daniel's well-reasoned advice went unheeded.

Daniel didn't realize perhaps that Ralph's desire to have him prepare reports didn't stem so much from executive need as from his wish to establish the principle of his command with the single most powerful employee in the company. He guessed that Ralph was just a well-meaning phoney who didn't respond to his reports because he wasn't knowledgeable in the field. Daniel was concerned about one thing; it was all right for Ralph to fool the office help about "the new dawn" as he had majestically called his rule, and it was one thing to fool customers, but if Ralph was fooling Steve, that was dangerous. Was Steve really as true a believer now as he was when Ralph had begun a year before?

Daniel grew restless. He decided to test Steve's credulity on Ralph's policies that very day at lunch.

Daniel casually remarked over espresso, "You think Ralph

can really deliver the sales forecast, Steve?"

Daniel listened as Steve waxed eloquent about Ralph's first-year performance. The big deals he closed. The big orders he'd written. The surging morale of the employees. Steve bubbled on, occassionally regaling himself with stories of Ralph's triumphs. It was true, Steve was still a believer, a year later.

Daniel left the resturant a shaken man. He felt Ralph would take Steve down and, with both of them, he would drown. Steve had some money to fall back on. Ralph would find another Steve in some big corporation somewhere. Only he, Daniel, would be 52, in a world where men of 42 struggled for good jobs. He sat up the night struggling with the alternatives. By morning, he boarded his commuter train deciding he had none. That day he resigned, protesting he was "tired, in need of a long rest." Steve pleaded with him to remain, offering him another raise, a 1-month vacation on the company. Daniel resisted these blandishments.

It took Daniel 6 weeks to relocate in a competitive company. He took less money but as he has since described, "The company president scrutinized my reports like geological surveys; sometimes he followed through and sometimes not, which at least meant to me that he was listening."

Ralph plucked a name ad agency, mail order genius to replace Daniel. He was forced to pay a staggering salary because Steve had grown terrified about losing mail business and was pressing him to "get the best." The name promoter didn't work out. He couldn't make his proven record in consumer mail pay off in trade mail. Steve, meanwhile, now watched the mail business stagger aimlessly downward while signing bigger and bigger salary and expense checks.

Ralph had again hit on a company problem of major importance, yet he again proposed a simplistic solution. Daniel's department was a company within a company, but his presence was not corrosive. Daniel's division sorely needed financial controls to help him plan promotions more effectively and to provide the company financial managers advance knowledge of his capital needs. His expenditures, although bringing successful results, imposed financial chaos on the company. Ralph was right; Daniel's work methods desperately needed changing. But he should have done that effectively. He should have read Daniel's reports. If he wanted a man to be responsible to him, he's got to be responsible. He was playing the army game with the company's most valuable employee—a game which eventually cost the company those valuable services.

Of course, there has yet to be a company which cannot survive without the services of any man. Yet, at the time, at the precise moment in Sunshine history when it needed Daniel's practiced hand on the complex and peculiar-to-the-industry type selling wheel, Ralph's misfire let it loose. Steve remained so sun-struck by Ralph's rosy pictures that he could not see any longer what his own timidity and desperation were doing to the company.

PROBLEM: Morale is sagging dangerously low.

Company morale was disastrously low. Fat pay increases had kept the plant and office quiet, but the worthwhile combat troops out there needed something startling to stir and energize them. Steve's reps were a beaten army.

SOLUTION: Boost it.

As he began his second year with sales below expectations, Ralph sensed a do-or-die situation just ahead. Morale was low. To stimulate it, Ralph desperately applied his Barnum instincts instead of his gut experience. So he decided to do it fast, do it big, and do it loud.

The company was long overdue for a national sales meeting. In the past, the previous owners had held a dry, flip chart, fly-in-fly-out, airport motel affair at which samples, prices, and stumbling speeches to sell more Sunnyboy products were distributed. Those meetings, Ralph concluded, were precisely what caused the sag in morale. Steve wasn't above a bit of show biz himself so Ralph's plan appealed to him. It also offered the essential element needed by Steve's mind to make it work, "wishing will make it so."

Ralph's Battle Plan was for a Supersonic Seminar by the Sea

in a rented villa at Cap d'Antibes on the French Riviera. Every operational manager, every sales representative and his wife were to be invited. He planned to charter a jumbo jet on a special deal, but it was finally blue-penciled by a trembling Steve as "a bit much." First-class fare round trip for the whole gang wasn't bad either. Once at the villa, the organization would be wined and dined and feted between seminars and then exposed to the product line in a spectacular musical presentation of the type Ralph ran when he worked for the $600,000,000-a-year company.

The producers of the show would create a musical comedy called "The Sunshine Shining Through" about the great prospects for the future of the company's new products and services. This was to be capped by a 4-day weekend on the Riviera during which the boys could luxuriate in the sun, gawk at the bikinied girls, gamble, tour, shop, eat and drink like nineteenth-century Romanoffs and fly home with a "Sunshine Smile and a Sunshine Glow."

Of course, the entire financial and business press would be invited. The story would make headlines in the *Wall Street Journal*. The meeting was budgeted to cost $100,000. As one must expect when taking nearly 150 people to the Riviera, the actual cost came in closer to $135,000. As a morale booster, it would be one hell of a vacation. Ralph justified the outrage on the basis that the regular ad budget was about $40,000, the regular meeting budget about $15,000, and the regular regional sales conference budget about $35,000. These three elements would be combined in one. For a lousy $10,000 more, look what kind of splash they could make. The damn thing would save the whole company.

For two essentially shrewd men like Ralph Oaks and my friend Steve to allow themselves to get so caught in this asinine, euphoric whirlpool of superhype indicates that the situation had so deteriorated that neither was able to think clearly at all anymore.

Steve and Ralph were now transformed. Steve was Louis B. Mayer and Ralph was Irving Thalberg. Together, they were making the greatest movie ever made, a spectacular production fabricated from ball-point pens, silk-screened T-shirts, imprinted rulers, inflatable life rafts, and slide rules which said: "Compliments of Sal's of the Sea, Steaks Lobsters—Catch Fresh Each Day."

In their Hollywood state of mind, Steve and Ralph were so busy orchestrating travel arrangements, discussing scripts and music with the show producers, casting and rehearsals that they totally forgot one small detail. The business. Everyone was so busy talking about the meeting, preparing for the meeting, meeting for the meeting that nobody was doing any work. Most of all, Steve and Ralph weren't doing any work. The offices of Sunshine became like a summer camp during Color War Week.

Finally, in the second week of that fateful July of that fateful year, the revelers left on a Sunday evening flight to the sunny shores of France to rebuild and relearn how lucky they were to be Sunshine people.

The production company had left two weeks earlier to make sure the show would be smack on the beam by the time the Sunshiners came. The producer assured Steve upon his arrival that everything would be performed to perfection—every line was right, every dance letter perfect, and every man in motion.

Ralph donned his sunglasses, his gondolier shirt, and shorts and began immediately working with the producers of the show to "check everything out." He became so entranced with the show biz part of the seminar that he hardly had time for the business at hand. During the first two days of "Get Acquainted" regional meetings, Ralph was busy getting acquainted with the show folk. He got acquainted with the production secretary; he got acquainted with the female vocalist, two dancers, and spent the second night on a nonstop pub crawl with the producer (an old army buddy) while Steve nervously shook hands with his people at a cocktail party, asking everyone in sight, "Hey, you seen Ralph?"

So while Steve stood helping hand out the howdy badges, Ralph disappeared. His howdy badge unpeeled, his bills mounting by the second, Steve resorted to his favorite escape route—the table. And he was in the right place. He sank into a miasma of gluttony, belching and hiccuping his way around the villa until 3 A.M., asking everyone, "Hey, you seen Ralph?"

A tom-catting Sales Vice President and a gluttonous President are not sights to inspire the participants to assume they'd been brought to this paradise to pursue serious work.

On the third morning, the business of the seminar began. The agenda called for an all-day sales seminar, dinner in the grand salon, the big musical company show, midnight supper at the villa, and a cruise to Monte Carlo on a leased yacht.

Into this day came, staggering and stumbling, sotty, bleary-eyed, wasted, belching, and farting, all the Sunshine men and women. On each one's table sat a thick loose-leaf binder containing the accumulated wisdom of ten weeks of intensive effort by dozens of people, pouring heart and soul into a documented analysis of company people, systems organization, products, goals, and strategies. In this ambiance of stupid, giggly lassitude, Steve soggily made his opening remarks. He welcomed everyone, modestly indicated he was a self-made man and a fighter of good fights. "I did not put my fortune into Sunshine to pull out rain!" he tested a pun. Everyone applauded. He introduced Ralph.

Barely able to stand, Ralph launched straight into the same sales pep talk he'd been giving for 25 years. He exhorted the audience to scale greater heights, "climb every mountain," paid tribute after tribute to Steve against a background of thunderous applause as the "far-seeing industrialist whose foresight has brought us together," and finally denounced, with evangelical fervor, the "prophets of doom" whose vision was jaded by contempt for "our great President, Stephen H. Baker."

Even Ralph's fatuous oratory couldn't compete with the Mediterranean. The villa's meeting room was the ballroom, which faced the dazzling blue sea. Through stately, 10-foot French windows, anyone in the audience could gaze at the magnificent coast, the glittering sands, the pink villas tucked like gems into the cliffsides. The azure sky and shimmering sapphire sea were one thing. The girls slinking across the beaches were another and, as they swayed half-nude on their appointed rounds, they beckoned the attention of the male contingent of the audience (about 95%). Ralph ended his remarks and was met by polite, distracted applause.

"Now, let's all turn to section one," Ralph's voice boomed out. It sounded like a country preacher leading a half-empty church in a hymn. Steve's composure broke. He suddenly felt a severe sensation of déjà vu. He had a premonition of incipient doom. Everything had fallen apart. The thought suddenly dawned on him—how would he pay for all this? Who was watching the store, if all the sales representatives were here? Who was out getting orders? What the hell was this all about? Steve began sweating hard. He became suddenly nauseous but held the vomit down with a belt of quinine water.

It was all over, maybe. But as long as he had them all there, in one room at the same time, he might as well maximize the opportunity. As Ralph reviewed company policies and products, Steve began scribbling furious notes on a small pad. During the luncheon break, Steve left the table after the turtle soup and was seen walking back and forth, violently gesturing with Ralph. After the lunch break, the people returned to the meeting room. But the expected presentation on product planning was suddenly postponed. Ralph arose and called for order.

"Ladies and gentlemen, your agenda indicates our next speaker was to be James Sidonia, on production planning. Before Jimmy talks, Steve, that is, Mr. Baker, would like a few minutes first." Ralph, visibly shaken, sat down, waving his hand toward Steve.

Steve stood up, his rotund frame suddenly squarish, direct, and menacing. He flipped the pages of his pad, looking grave. The audience sensed his mood and stiffened to attention. Nudges awoke the drowsers in the back rows. Whispering stopped. All eyes were riveted on Steve as he began.

"Hey you, Walt Cooke, how many colors do we offer in our walnut desk set line?" he shot out.

Cooke reddened and fumbled.

"You, Ed Quinlan, why can we service the Chicago trade faster than Acme, without a showroom at the Merchandise Mart?"

Another embarrassed silence.

Steve continued around the room like a prosecutor. Looking down only occasionally at his notes, he blasted sharp, pointed, appropriate questions to about 60 of the 100 people assembled. About one person in ten had any intelligent answers. For the remaining four hours, the meeting dramatically turned around. Shirts were opened, drapes were drawn, lights turned on, seminar books read, questions and answers exchanged, informative, vital dialogue ensued. Steve, however, was not consoled.

As the meeting adjourned, the men congratulated Ralph and other people from the home office on the "dramatic coup." They thought the whole thing was staged. They thought it was some superadvanced meeting technique rooted in psychodrama. Ralph knew better but wisely played along. Now he was buttonholing everyone, "Hey, you seen Steve?" Nobody had. Steve had slipped out to his suite. Within the following hour he had issued a statement to be mimeoed at once.

> FROM: *Steven Baker*
> TO: *All Concerned*
> RE: *Seminar*
> The seminar is cancelled effective **6** P.M. tonight. We will not be responsible for any bills incurred beyond lodging tonight. Plane tickets to New York, Chicago, and Los Angeles have been arranged and are at the desk. Strongly advise you to check out tonight if you can and take advantage of the special bus I have chartered for the airport. Plane reservations have been changed from first class to coach. Any change back will be charged to your personal account.

A stunned staff began milling around the great hall downstairs. Many were without sufficient money to chance getting stuck another day. The charter buses were jammed. By 10 A.M. the next day, the villa was empty.

During the two weeks that followed the Cap d'Antibes fiasco, relations between Ralph and Steve froze. It was now a race between Ralph resigning or getting canned. Ralph beat out Steve by a few days.

The two men enjoyed a farewell drink in Steve's office. Ralph kept calling Steve "guy," and Steve kept calling Ralph "guy." Both were happy to be out of each other's way. Within two months, Ralph joined a famous aerospace company to head up a new consumer division. The Ralph Oakses of this world will always survive. Steve joined another select company—the legions of the busted. Sunshine Industries was dead.

AUTOPSY

It was Steve, of course, not Ralph Oaks, who murdered the company. Everyone knows that in the early stages of a disease, it is very difficult to diagnose but reasonably easy to cure: that in the advanced stages of a disease, it is a snap to diagnose but sheer murder to cure. Steve did not apply this common-sense principle to his company.

Steve should have smelled something rotten in Underwriter Hayes' assurances that he could buy a company under its asset value, when it earned good profits, simply because the owner had a stroke. It was too facile. Steve was too smart to have swallowed whole a story like that.

Once he bought the business, he neglected it as long as it was still making money. When it declined, he panicked; and instead of calmly trying to diagnose its problems, he ran for the nearest savior.

Steve believed in Ralph because he desperately wanted to believe in someone. When he saw he'd bought a lemon, his survival instincts knew only one course: Find a savior. A man accustomed to early success can't cope with failure as well as a man who's been down a few times.

Steve bought all the easy answers Ralph was selling because they appealed to his emotional needs, not his common sense. In his own beginnings, Steve had won his stripes by outperforming tired old men, and Ralph's energetic image appealed to Steve's notion of success. Ralph knew that bosses liked the direct, military approach to business problems. He was expert at talking and acting like what he was doing was getting results. Steve stubbornly rejected dozens of alternatives to explain his business's decline, because Ralph, in his Joe College, R.O.T.C. way, kept telling him what he wanted to hear and not what he needed to know.

All the Ralph Oakses of the world, real or phoney, cannot by themselves, save a dying business. Ralph was, like any other competent front office man, a good politician. His basic expertise was in winning pay increases every year. It mattered little to Ralph whether he worked for Sunshine or Moonshine. It mattered little what he sold—computers, farm equipment, cosmetics, advertising specialities, premiums, jet air frames. An ordinary politician runs on his record. A great one, like Ralph, runs on his politics— what he stands for, his personal presence, his attitudes, his image, not his know-how. Steve should have known that. He had no right to expect more from Ralph than what he got. He wanted a "high-powered guy" and that was Ralph. He knew how to sell the big order once, whom to pay off, whom to drink with, which guy wants to get laid, and which buzz words motivate salesmen.

A business in trouble is a bundle of problems that simply can't be solved by bringing in a Messiah. Nothing ever replaces the hard-nosed, serious business of admitting mistakes, putting them in the past, and redirecting the energies of the business with groups of people working in concert. Relying on the sainted miracles of one man cannot save the business. Even if he happens to be as brilliantly gifted as you.

3

An American Dream—Jonathan Edwards'
Bum Steer

THE PURITAN ETHIC, of all Western man's great ideas, has the unique distinction of being the simultaneous enemy and ally of every small businessman in America. It is his sturdy ally when his dogged pursuit of his goals against all odds propels his young business ahead through shaky times. It is his enemy when he believes that it can bring him everything.

What this system of beliefs does not provide, is that which it could never provide: a sense of the limitations life imposes on even the luckiest and pluckiest. The Great Puritan American Dream, so enriched by "the sky's the limit" mentality, encourages belief in the impossible. A true believer is not prepared to understand his personal limitation and often stumbles quickly from the American Dream into a nightmare.

It should surprise no one that there are millions of men who've worked from sunrise to sunset, performed extraordinary financial miracles, traded fairly with their peers, and gone broke. There are millions of people who slave away at miserable jobs, hoping for a "break," all their lives. They go to church every week. They believe. They tell the truth. Then when confronted with the relentless tales of success of less virgin souls, they either grow bitter, or more likely, "hand it" to the guy who made it on the sharp underside.

We do not suggest that people stop believing in the American Way. We do suggest that they believe only part of it.

The most common small-business blunder and the one which is most deeply rooted in the American Puritan Ethic is the deadly game of Overreach. Overreach is born of the systematic cultivation of the Puritan Ethic at its purest. It's the unshakable loyalty and faith in the idea that in America:

1]   A good thing can be expanded infinitely, because if it's good, everyone will want to try it.
2]   The sky's the limit when you respect your elders, salute the flag, are faithful to your wife, and go to church every week.
3]   Success breeds success.

As this case history demonstrates, it ain't necessarily so.

Jonathan Edwards, one of our earliest and most Puritan of early settlers, said: "Resolved, never to do anything which I should be afraid to do if it were the last hour of my life." His fearless defiance, chiseled deeply into his portraits, lived within the mind and body of a shy, skinny kid from upstate New York named Wayne Evans. In contrast to Edwards and other righteous-looking Puritans, Wayne looked meek, passive, crumpled. When he showed up at the U.S. Marines Recruiting Office in the small city of his birth, in 1942, the sergeant on duty was unimpressed with the mousy kid with the shock of chestnut hair and told him to wait till he was drafted.

Wayne did, and was, in 1942. Before too many months had passed, he was fighting with Patton in North Africa. He was one of those raw draftees who acquitted himself nobly in battle by being part of the group who didn't panic at the first exposure to enemy fire. His unit later moved into Europe, participating in the final dagger thrust into the heart of Hitler Germany. Decorated, rested, and shipped home fresh, Wayne Evans faced a 1945 America, waiting with arms open wide to embrace him and all the other young men who defended freedom against tyranny. What could a grateful country do for this son of a railroad switchman with a fifth-grade education?

There was the GI Bill. That was not Wayne's way. The part of Jonathan Edwards that lived inside was not interested in books. He knocked around the cities of upstate New York and New England for nearly 6 years without much success. But he had faith. He finally settled in Bright City, New York, as a small appliance repair man for a small chain of stores. Bright City was international headquarters of a national manufacturer of electrical equipment and, for its huge assembly plants, drew unskilled workers from a pool all over the nation.

In the same year, a pretty young lady of 22, from a Georgia dirt farm, came to Bright City seeking work at one of the big electrical plants. Sally Rowan had left behind a desolate life which included a drunken husband and his six wretched children from a previous marriage.

Months after her arrival, Sally had also put down roots. She'd found work as a solderer-trainee in the plant. She kept a tiny, but impeccably neat, apartment in a modestly respectable, clapboard rooming house in a nice part of town. She saw lots of respectable young men socially, but none reached her standard. Sally would not fall into a repeat of a previous error; she would not marry until she knew her man was a "mover."

Sally met Wayne Evans one weekend about six months after they'd both hit town. Sally's television set fritzed out the same day a favorite old Spencer Tracy movie was being played and she was desperately trying to get Wayne's boss to send a man out to fix it. Wayne's boss pleaded that all his men were out on jobs, that it would be impossible for him to get to her until the following day.

Wayne overheard the conversation. He'd picked up the habit of listening in because his boss always asked callers for their name, number, and set model before he'd talk to them. Wayne made his living fixing irons, toasters, and pressure cookers, but he'd tinkered with TV on the side through a correspondence school course. He'd decided, when he'd gained enough nerve, to ask to take on TV repair, then still an esoteric speciality.

This was his chance to test himself out. "Darn dame is crazy," the boss said, slamming the phone down on the cradle. "Worried about some old Spencer Tracy movie on tonight." Wayne's boss left the desk to walk up front to greet a customer who'd walked into the store. Wayne memorized the number. "Goin' out to lunch," he said, walking out the back, the number and name branded in his head.

He got to a public phone, called Sally, told her he was the television repair man and that he could come over that evening at 5:30. Sally was relieved.

Wayne arrived on time at Sally's chintz-curtained little

apartment. The earnest young man was led to the television set, taking full notice of the attractive and, to all appearances, single young lady who was his first TV client. He tinkered feverishly a few minutes. As the first beads of worried sweat began rolling down his forehead, he located the problem; it was a simple tube replacement. He opened his box of tubes provided by the correspondence school, made the change, and presto, the set was operating perfectly. One had to understand the world of television viewing in 1952 to fully appreciate the sense of relief a set owner felt when the repairman fixed the set on the spot, turned it on, and a bright, sharp picture blew onto the screen. The dreaded, "I dunno, she'll hafta go back to the shop" was like telling someone they had a terminal disease.

Relieved and overjoyed, Sally asked how much. Equally relieved that the problem wasn't something one lesson ahead of his progress in the course, Wayne declined the offer of payment, saying it was "on the house."

"You must have a nice boss," she said. "He didn't sound very nice on the phone."

After some casual conversation, Sally invited the young man to sit down for some beer. Wayne took the offer. She told the story of the Spencer Tracy movie. The evening wore on, and Wayne moved the subject into his own war experiences, his hard six years banging around from job to job and his new-found determination to make it in the world of TV repair.

"All you need is these," he said, lifting his wiry arms and clenching his fists, "and a little of this," pointing to his head. "That's all you need in this country. Believe it, Sally."

She did. It was what she'd been wanting to hear. They watched the movie together. They began dating. Wayne eventually confessed about his bogus TV repair call. Sally told him in terrible detail about growing up in rural Georgia, the too-early marriage, and her determination to "make it up." It was a warm, balmy, beautiful May night that Wayne led Sally to a credit jewelry store and picked out an engagment ring. That Christmas they were married in his church and moved into her apartment.

Wayne had graduated into regular TV repairman. His ambition now focused on opening a repair shop on his own. The apartment was adequate but crowded. Wayne was pushed even harder when Sally told him she was pregnant. He began looking around for a location.

The city was now glutted with opportunistic young repairmen, many of them graduates of the big factory school at the plant. Undaunted by the competition, Wayne took a small store on North Avenue, knowing somehow that a God-fearing American who believed and worked hard must prevail. But it was not so easy. Wayne found his fair price "service with an All-American Smile" policy did not mean as much as his ability to attract new customers. His meager take from the shop was simply not enough to keep wife and new baby girl in food and rent. He found a part-time job at the old Owl's Nest Diner on Route 101, just outside the city. Phil Leary, who owned the small, lively eatery was nearing 70 and could no longer run the place alone with an ailing wife to look after and a short-order cook who drank heavily.

Phil hired Wayne to assist during the peak evening truck-stop hours. Wayne washed floors, filled the napkin boxes and the sugar bowls, waited on tables, washed dishes, and was soon throwing a nifty sunnyside egg. An understanding Phil allowed his young helper to bolt out the door whenever the phone rang, announcing a TV service call from the shop.

Wayne was dragging after several months of these 14-hour days, but the slow liquidation of his debts and increase in disposable income pleased him immensely. He lingered over one chore at the Owl's Nest Diner every night—that was dusting clean the American flag that hung over the cash register. He believed.

Leary's short-order cook sobered up long enough to trek 250 miles south to New York City one weekend to take a job at a busy midtown luncheonette paying $25 a week more. Leary asked Wayne if he wanted the cook's job. He promised to teach him everything. He promised to meet whatever he was earning from the shop plus his part-time wages and tips if he'd agree.

Wayne discussed Leary's offer with Sally. The hours were longer, the work harder. But there were other compensations. He was naturally adept with food; he'd learn a good skill and, when the demand for TV repairmen increased, he could always go back to tinkering. Sally was only displeased by the thought of Wayne not utlizing his training as a skilled repairman, of wasting his time making hot cakes and beef stew. Wayne said that all work was

God's work and that net after taxes would be $12 per week more and that was good enough for him. Wayne closed the shop, stored his tools in the basement of the rooming house, and donned his white apron.

During the following three years, Wayne learned everything he thought there was to know about running a little roadside diner. Leary knew this too and kept Wayne's wages fairly tied to his own annual profit and loss statement.

In 1956, Leary was nearing his 75th birthday, his wife was now gone, and he decided to live out his years with his daughter on her husband's small Vermont farm. He offered the Owl's Nest to Wayne at a fair price, agreeing to take no cash, but notes only over a 2-year period. Wayne quickly agreed. He now applied the principle that in America, those who wanted to sweat hard, work hard, tow the mark, shoot square, love mother, flag, God, and country could do no wrong in business.

He moved to a decrepit bungalow 50 yards from the diner. Sally characteristically spruced up the place into a little *True Romances* "dream cottage" with lots of ingenuity and J. C. Penney's home décor specials.

Wayne, for the first time in his life, owned something. It gave him time to think. He once again turned to the source of all knowledge in America, the back pages of comic books. He noticed an ad while reading *Amazing Comics* one evening: LAPORTE EXTENSION COLLEGE URGES AMBITIOUS YOUNG MEN TO PROGRESS IN THE BUSINESS WORLD. EARN UP TO $200 A WEEK KNOWING THE SECRETS OF BIG BUSINESS. Wayne subscribed to courses in accounting, in salesmanship, and in business organization. Becoming a possessor of the knowledge that "the line and staff system of organization is the most eminently adaptable management technique yet passed from the military to the corporate world" did not, of course, help him improve the sales of tomato surprise over chicken and brown rice. Our culture is so inexplicably positive, however, about the way anything can be adapted by anyone, that even though Wayne's slavish intensity to self-improvement misfired, it had the desired effects anyway. These essentially worthless courses forced Wayne to begin thinking beyond the fifteen hours a day from breakfast to the midnight special. He began to think about the importance of things—that cleanliness was crucial in a food business, that value and quality were a delicate balance. So at the end of his first year as owner of the Owl's Nest, Wayne Evans could look proudly at any man and feel he ran a good, wholesome business with a growing reputation in the area.

As the second year began, he now waited for his long, grueling hours of work and study to pay off. He expanded the diner to six more stools and waited for lightning to strike. And it did. Literally.

That April, a violent electrical storm struck the region. Local rivers overflowed, power lines crashed down and flooding ensued; people were cut off without food or fresh water. Red Cross and military units were closing in on the area, but until their arrival, the State Police had organized an emergency command station and shelter a half-mile up the road from the Owl's Nest in the high school.

Wayne had removed Sally and his daughter from the bungalow to the higher ground of the diner when the storm had broken hours before. He was busy assembling booths together for his wife and child to sleep in when a State policeman knocked at his door. He rubbed away the moisture from inside the window and saw the friendly face in the window. He opened up. A tall, husky State policeman walked in.

"Saw your sign. Say, sir, we've got an emergency station set up over there at the high school. You wouldn't have any food left, would you?"

Wayne was dumbstruck. "How'd you see my sign? All the power's been down for hours!"

The policeman smiled. "Maybe its fate, brother, I dunno, but there she is," he said, pointing outside the window. Sure enough, miraculously, through some incredibly crossed wire, the large neon sign OWL'S NEST DINER EATS was blinking. It was the only light on anywhere for hundreds of yards.

It was a sign. It was an omen. Of that Wayne was certain, but how? He turned to the trooper. "I'll get some things together. Give me a few minutes."

Wayne had a very large roast beef he'd cooked that evening for the following day's lunch business. He wrapped it with clean towels, grabbed a long loaf of bread and a pot of gravy, and

motioned to the trooper to "lead the way." Loaded down with
the food, Wayne followed the trooper to the radio car. They
drove up the road to the school building where a hungry platoon
of troopers and relief workers awaited them.

Wayne set to work at once. He reheated the large roast in
the school cafeteria oven. He spread out a cheerful, red table-
cloth atop a section of a long, wooden plank supported by two
sawhorses. He organized himself, smiling at those who began
gathering around him, and began slicing the roast. The hot,
steaming slices of meat rose like perfume to the nostrils of the
famished contingent. Wayne glanced up. He saw from the lengthening line now forming along the wall that he'd never have
enough bread to make enough sandwiches. And there was none
left at the diner. So he made do. He sliced the beef in large, thin
pieces and laid them over one slice of bread split in halves,
poured the steaming gravy over, wedged in a thick slice of pickle,
and served it all up on paper plates with hot, steaming mugs of
coffee and hot chocolate.

The ravenous horde of volunteers gobbled the sandwiches
like ambrosia. Wayne lingered a few hours accepting the thanks
and compliments of the crowd. "Come by the diner," he said.
"Bring the family for the Sunday Turkey Dinner special." Dozens
of people remembered that night. Long after the storm was a
memory, people began streaming into the Owl's Nest on Sunday
afternoons. But they didn't order the turkey dinner. They asked
for Wayne's special, "The Split Roast Beef" Sandwich. One
trooper who was fed by Wayne that night came in one day and
asked for the "Emergency" Roast Beef Special. And so it was
named. Wayne embellished the dish with a choice of mashed or
french fries and, within three months of the great storm, was
doing a brisk business in the now popular Emergency Beef Special, a real bargain for 90¢, with potatoes, pickle, lettuce,
tomatoes, and cole slaw.

By 1959, the Owl's Nest could been seen from miles down
the road, its blinking 10-foot-long sign shouting "Home of the
E-Mergency Beef King-Size Sandwich." At year's end, Wayne
had broken the $100,000 mark in gross sales and showed a net
before taxes of $18,000, after taking $15,000 in salaries for himself and his wife. This bolt of righteous good fortune could not

have come to a "Godless communist," in Wayne's view, but only
to a man who had slaved as he had—at the altar of free enterprise
and clean living.

Wayne instinctively sensed the onrush of specialization in
the bursting world of fast food. He saw new pizza parlors, hamburger and chicken stands, and soft ice cream castles popping up
all along Highway 101. He reasoned that if he continued to add
stools and seating capacity to his diner, he'd, by necessity, be
forced to continually expand his menu offerings. His sales checks
revealed the overwhelming, runaway leader was his special roast
beef sandwich. "Anyone can fry an egg," he told Sally one night.
"But not everyone can make my roast beef gravy." And he was
right. Wayne followed his instincts because their companion,
walking beside them, was his appointment with a destiny created
out of his iron beliefs.

With borrowed capital, Wayne demolished the old place,
bought the land under it from a local farmer, and built King Beef
Palace, which opened in 1961. His correspondence school business courses had impressed him with the need to use expertise,
and since all his life, he respected "real American know-how," he
brought in a fast food expert from California he'd read about in
a trade magazine to design his Palace as a bunkhouse dining
room with Western ranch motif. Above the main doors a 5-foot,
plaster Black Angus head beneath which were two American
flags greeted the thousands of patrons from a fifty mile radius
who now thronged to King Beef for Wayne's famous speciality.
Wayne's success enabled him to move out into the wider business
and social community of the county. He joined a local Republican
Club and, actively participated in Rotary, Chamber of Com-
merce, and several religious and charity groups. He especially
enjoyed the Chamber dinners, after which leading businessmen
of the community stood up in bloated praise of the system which
had been good to them all.

It was at this time, during this heady, bubbling mix of men
on the move, men of wealth, and men of would-be wealth, that
he began to believe that nothing on God's earth could stop him
from making millions on his very special way of serving a roast
beef sandwich.

In 1964, King Beef Palace #2 opened on the north side of

the city, 25 miles away, to service the southbound highway traffic and draw customers from the slowly filling northern suburban areas. King Beef #2 was an instantaneous success.

Wayne's banker and fellow Chamber brother continuously urged him ahead. Wayne's community standing, his record of solid integrity, and good cash balance were worth a line of credit high enough to consider a King Beef Palace #3 the following year. All the intoxicants began mixing in Wayne's head. "Why wait? Why not now?" Wayne responded to the offer. "Well, well, why not!" The banker replied in his best Edward Arnold style.

The results of success now changed the Evanses' life style. They had long moved from the bungalow to a modest cottage in a good suburb, but with the opening and quick success of King Beef #3, in Old Mill, Connecticut, the Evanses now moved into a sprawling, old colonial mansion on 2 acres in the city's most snobbish suburb. Along with the house all the accoutrements—the maid, the swimming pool, the private schools for his two daughters, and the frequent shopping trips down to New York or over to Boston by Sally whenever the mood struck her. Wayne's belief in the American dream was now fully redeemed. Wasn't he living it every day?

He'd still arise early every day, pull out of his driveway in a sleek luxury sedan, drive twenty minutes to his office above King Beef #1, go through his mail, talk to his three managers, check the previous day's sales reports, discuss prices with his purchasing man, and take off for a run around his three restuarants.

No matter which King Beef Palace he visited that day, he saw a restaurant lined three deep with people; a jammed parking lot; ringing cash registers; a whirling, churning, but well-ordered excitement. The public appreciated Wayne's commitment to quality food served at a clean place at the right price. His managers and employees called him "Uncle Wayne." He'd have a smile for everyone and a silver dollar for any kid in the restaurant who came up and recognized him. He read register tapes that built like great skyscrapers—every day of the week, every month of the year, every year—bigger, higher and better.

But Wayne could don the martinet's scowl at will. He insisted on clean, immaculate premises and on clean, immaculate people. To assure his kind of people only worked at his establishments, he personally interviewed every one, down to the part-timers who swept the floors and took out the garbage. Most of his help were college students, friends of his children, or worthies selected from rolls at the Chamber. The whole white, crew-cutted, soft-spoken, fresh-from-the-shower crew were, indeed, in every sense, a family. They were a perfect extension of the mind and emotions of Wayne Evans, at his best and at his worst.

In 1963, when Wayne's three palaces had reached the healthy combined gross of $175,000 per month, he was convinced that all those articles he'd been reading in the business press were true; America was hungry and getting hungrier. And he was convinced the nation was infinitely hungry for his roast beef. So with his friend the banker at his side, Wayne Evans, who 11 years before was fixing steam irons at $1.75 an hour, began to dream a bigger dream. He hired a consultant to appraise his business and make recommendations about expanding it into a national operation.

The consultant spent 10 grueling weeks studying Wayne's business. His study finished, the consultant joined Wayne at poolside one sunny August afternoon to deliver a capsule of his final recommendations. Here were his findings:

1] Wayne undoubtedly had an gold mine. His food was excellent; hygiene way above average; his people efficient, warm, and bright. But the hard truth was that all these assets would eventually be eroded to some degree by rising food prices and by a diminishing unskilled labor supply which were natural outgrowths of expansion far from home base. If he could continue keeping distribution and management costs low, he could maintain profitability without debasing food quality. That was the trick.

2] Wayne was unquestionably aware of the fact that roast beef fast food operations were springing up all over the nation. Many of these were operated by skilled franchise operators, who were extremely well-heeled and, sooner or later, his King Beef Palace expansions would run head to head against real competition. In

Wayne's little part of earth, there was no competition at all.

3]   Much of Wayne's success stemmed from its tightly controlled local geography. Customers knew Wayne. He was seen very often at all his places, smiling at kids, distributing silver dollars, dressed in his cowboy suit, even waiting on tables. There was no way to reproduce that kind of asset value across a large string of restaurants. Wayne could not be entirely sure that a large regional operation throughout the Northeast would not lose by thinning out his local magic.

4]   Wayne was, of course, cognizant of the fact that franchising fast food was essentially a real estate game. Outside his local area, he might be forced to bid against other fast food people for prime locations. Spotting hidden gems would require his retaining a highly skilled real estate department manager, whose recommendations needed to be acted upon with lightning speed. That meant plenty of capital to react quickly.

The consultant ended by saying: "Mr Evans, you have a helluva good business here. If you operate it another ten years or so, it will probably make you a very rich man. Fast food franchising is exploding right now, but it will take a rapid capital pump and a lightning fast assembly of a professional management team to maintain the King Beef volume per unit you presently enjoy. It's not impossible, but its not easy."

The consultant concluded his remarks by strongly recommending that Wayne stick to his three Palaces for the time being and leave the battle to the big boys. He also suggested that if Wayne was so eager to pump more capital into his business, he would be well advised to consider several offers he'd already received from blue-chip, national fast food operators to buy him out and give him everything he'd need to expand at the same time.

Wayne was scandalized. He respected expertise alright, but only when it matched his preconceived ideas. Didn't this guy know how well fast food places were doing?

Didn't he know the figures on Americans eating out? Why should he sell out? Why wasn't the sky the limit for him as well as the big boys? The consultant did know it all. What he tried to explain to Wayne was Wayne's own success. He tried to make Wayne see that certain vital ingredients of that success were not reproducible on a large scale. He could be dead wrong, he said, but that was his opinion. He felt Wayne could expand to a fourth, possibly a fifth, restaurant out of the area to test the premise without risking a large, rolling expansion.

Wayne coolly thanked the man for his help. He grudgingly paid him $5,000 for the study. It could have been the best $5,000 he'd ever spent, but Wayne's beliefs, his devotion to the precepts of never say quit, had hardened into canonical law. He would not be kept tucked away among the foothills of upper New York by a college professor. He pressed ahead.

It seemed clear to him that no magic formula existed for fast food success. Any of the major chains were no smarter than he was. They used the leverage of money; so could he. They needed brains—they bought them; so could he. It was a free country.

After an intense search to find a compatible franchising manager (someone who shared his evangelical beliefs in doing the impossible), he set out upon a 3-month tour of the entire Northeast from Maine down to Washington. With an abundance of fast food franchises floating around like soap bubbles at a kindergarten recess, Wayne was bound to get bogged down. Instead of finding potential franchisees willing to take his generous deal, he was rebuffed at every turn. When he did find willing ears, he and his manager often became stuck in lengthy, frustrating, nit-picking negotiations with small-town lawyers. Most of these forays fizzled. Rather than return home to think things through, Wayne quixotically jumped into the breech himself. He would show these nonbelievers. He decided to swing all the way himself. He would open seven more owned-and-operated King Beef Palaces on his own.

He arranged financing through several banks, calling many markers among friends in the process. He took mortgages and collateralized all his personal assets—his houses, his stocks and bonds. Against the advice of his closest friends, he plunged headlong into action with designers, realty site assemblers, and a new management staff gleaned from name fast food operations at high salaries.

Wayne selected sites from the southern shore of Maryland to northwestern New York. He opened two King Beefs in 1965, three more in 1966, four in 1967 and stopped to survey his little kingdom. It was a monumental task, but it was done—11 Palaces in total. All opened without a dime of public capital. All planned and executed and run by a staff hired and trained by Wayne.

His approach made sturdy sense. He'd pass one full month personally at each new location to assure as smooth a launch as possible during the traditionally trying shakedown period. At each site, when Wayne was completely satisfied that the manager and staff knew their responsibilities, he proceeded to the next location. But the rug was beginning to roll up behind him. His new locations were hastily assembled. Local meat suppliers were inconsistent in quality; many did not meet Wayne's precise standards. Counter personnel, while on their best behavior during Wayne's presence, slacked off fast when he left, were fired, and replaced with increasing frequency.

Wayne was totally unequipped to handle rapid labor turnover. He'd been accustomed to hiring each person himself. He'd been spoiled by the singular situation of having the sons and daughters of his country club friends working for him at the original three units around his home city. At all new locations, many of the youngsters scoffed at what they believed were Wayne's archaic notions about "neat appearance." To Wayne, King Beefs were palaces of righteousness; to many of his newer employees, they were places to grind out a few extra dollars.

Wayne's unit managers made valiant efforts to avoid hiring "long hairs, freaks, and hippies" (Wayne's catchall for any young person with hair below the ears), but they failed. They forced Wayne to relent. He did, later pointing to the high rate of turnover as proof of his contention that they were not only ruining the nation but directly responsible for the lackluster performance of many of his new sites. Wayne's frustrations mounted and receipts in all eight of his new operations dropped by the month. At the close of 1967, Wayne's company broke even, only because his original three hometown spots made so much money.

As he sat poring over his 1967 operating results, his heart

wrenched. Two of his 11 places did not even pay their way on rent and labor. They were bleeding every other place dry. He could not understand how and where his faith and diligence had failed him. Like Abraham sacrificing Isaac, he tearfully ordered the two weakest links in his chain shut—but a gracious and omnipotent God did not appear to assure him that it was merely a test of faith. The 2 palaces were boarded up.

With nine places left, Wayne determined to redouble his efforts. He now began to exercise the great American practice of high-speed promotion. He tried clowns, family days at half price, TV commercials featuring himself on a white horse, car giveaways, and hidden treasure events. But no amount of promotional muscle could solve what was essentially plaguing King Beef: There was only one Wayne to go around. His local managers were so busy running carnivals, attending local Chamber and club meetings, sponsoring Little League teams that they became preoccupied and neglected the business. Sanitation deteriorated, food quality suffered, and personnel problems persisted.

In 1968, Wayne once more agonized over his operating statement. The unavoidable conclusions were dancing across the work sheets like tiny devils. He reluctantly gave in to intense pressure from his accountants and agreed to close four more locations. And now there were five—his original three (still bringing in the biggest profits) and two outside his home grounds.

To a man of Wayne's set of mind, the middle 1960's was a time of chaos. Even the election of a more conservative President in 1968 could do little more than offer Wayne small comfort. He was convinced that the long hairs, hippies, and freaks were out to do in hard work, devotion to the good things of life, family, flag, and country. The central issue, which Wayne refused to face, was that the public outside his home city simply didn't feel that his roast beef was so superior to the half-dozen other roast beef places from which they could choose. They had no historical or emotional ties to King Beef; they had no loyalty or sense of "family" drawing them to Wayne's Palaces. And Wayne couldn't be every place all the time to watch over his business. It is fair to say that he had been warned.

Wayne was now in deep trouble. Once again forced to the wall, Wayne sold off his two remaining out-of-state locations to a soft ice cream chain, reducing him to his original three home-town locations. It was now 1970, and the credit crunch was on. Wayne was asked by his bankers to have a hard look at his current situation.

Wayne had absorbed a total beating of over $1,000,000 counting construction, advertising expenses, broken leases, construction deals, and various purveyor lawsuits. He sought refuge in his original three Palaces. His hands burned, Wayne wanted to return home to hearth, family, and friends and never wander again. But his troubles, it seemed, were only beginning.

He'd extended himself at several banks with loans for his expansion program collateralized by personal assets and, of course, the properties for which the capital was expended. The banks looked over his books and politely asked Wayne to please retire half the principal on the outstanding notes over the following 90-day period. Principal and interest together ran over $700,000. Wayne huddled with his accountants. If he retired the notes in that period of time, he would be effectively broke for the following several years because he would be forced to borrow privately to continue running the three resturants into order to meet the notes.

However, part of his loan was collateralized by personal assets. Were he to default, the banks, friends or not, would be forced to seize his assets in payment.

Wayne confronted the bankers with a plan. Could they renew his notes for another year? He'd pay all interest, of course, and try to retire half the principal that year (1970) and half in 1971. The banks thought about the plan. It seemed reasonable. The weekend following, Wayne met his closest banker friend at the club. Wayne had casually remarked he had received an offer for the Palaces from a national chain and refused it. The banker asked how much? Wayne replied he thought he could have gotten close to a million. The banker exploded. He chastised Wayne for dismissing such a generous offer out of hand. Had he not thought of his obligations to the bank? To himself and his friends?

Astounded by the banker's reaction, Wayne grimly left the club, seething with anger. He was more determined than ever to make it through on his own. He called the banks the following Monday advising them he intended to clean up all his debts in 90 days, interest, principal and all. He then went to a private investor who agreed to lend Wayne $350,000 in operating capital in exchange for a 40% interest in the business.

Wayne worked fifteen-hour days again over the next five months. He did not meet all the notes on time, but his banks, seeing he was cleaning his way through, gave him 30-day extensions. He was, at least, free of all debt by early 1972. His new partner's notions about business, however, sharply differed from his. The man had made millions in industrial feeding. He wanted to exploit the reputation of King Beef in that field. Wayne stubbornly resisted. The man offered to buy Wayne out. Wayne furiously countered that he would buy the caterer out. "With what?" the caterer said. "You don't have a pot to piss in, Wayne." That awful, telling, and unfortunately on-the-mark riposte destroyed Wayne. It was true. All he had left were his interest in the business, his house, and what was left of his stock portfolio.

Wayne went back to the banks. Once again, his unyielding hope in goodness as he saw it lifted him into a dream world of salvation on the wings of a red, white, and blue eagle. The bank agreed to back Wayne's wish to extricate himself from the partnership. The caterer demanded $500,000 for his share. Wayne reported this to the bank. The bank agreed but demanded all of Wayne's personal assets as collateral, plus the restaurants themselves. Wayne hesitatingly agreed. He bought the man out. It cost him $150,000. His way of life had now run up an impossible tab. His family brought pressure on him. Sally would not live a day longer in that house knowing it was mortgaged up to its attics. She could not face anyone at the club. Her older daughter working at a local department store was evidence to local society that the Evanses were indeed, as everyone suspected, dead broke.

Once again, Wayne was in a race to keep a step ahead of the banks. He finally broke under the pressure. He contacted the chain. They had recently opened a successful new outlet of their own not far from Wayne's Palace #1. Their interest had flagged. Now getting desperate, Wayne worked feverishly to sell out his interests.

Once again, he found his old partner, the industrial feeder. The man offered Wayne an all-cash deal of $600,000. Wayne bit hard and took it. He repaid the bank which left him $450,000 before taxes. After taxes (and Wayne was involved for nearly three months in dispute with his Uncle Sam about certain liberties he'd taken with the tax laws), Wayne left his business with about $100,000 by the time his creditors had plucked him.

It is a fitting close to our little tale that we now report that Wayne's faith in the system, while shaken, was not dead. He left the city with his family and nearly $400,000 which included the proceeds from the sale of his house and journeyed out West where he met a man of similar viewpoint.

The man urged Wayne to sink his money into a family motel-resturant operation in a retirement community in the great sun belt. Reborn, renewed, and refreshed by the still bubbling vitality of the growth ethic in the southwest, Wayne went in. Wayne's unremitting faith was grotesquely rewarded when, after a short time, the venture fizzled, taking with it nearly two-thirds of Wayne's capital.

He has since moved with his family to Texas where he works as a manager of a pleasant steak house outside a large city. A business associate was in that town not too long ago and stopped in for a steak. He greeted Wayne warmly and they passed a convivial evening. Wayne, I am told, is still convinced he was done in by the long hairs, the hippies, and the freaks.

My friend tells me he that stayed there until closing. He said good-bye to Wayne, who, in the semidarkness, seated among all the tables with chairs piled on them, was reading a franchising magazine "chock full of hundreds of money making ideas for men who are willing to work." As my friend closed the door, he peered through the glass. There was Wayne, energetic as ever, busily tearing out coupons and scribbling them in with his stubby, headwaiter-manager's pencil.

It was true. He still believes.

AUTOPSY

During a man's lifetime, he confronts many positive beliefs. Those to which he stubbornly clings, despite the recurrence of grim experience and life in a widended world, are generally child-

hood fantasies which never die easily. Grownups reject or cling
to what parents believe, but they can't remain impassive about
them. A man born into a pious family grows up either pious or,
just as often, agnostic. It is the emotional heat and turbulence in
his parents and the sting of repetitive dogma which molds attitudes of children in iron.

Among those attitudes which pervaded the early penurious
childhood of Wayne Evans was the Puritan Ethic cum American
Dream. The notions cultivated in his mind by his struggling
family were deeply rooted in the expansive railroading stories his
father told the Evans children on bitter winter nights. He filled
their ears with tales of financial derring-do, of great figures of a
golden era, like Daniel Drew, Diamond Jim Brady, the old Com-
modore Vanderbilt, the Goulds, the Harrimans, all the robber
barons who by "luck and pluck" built the nation's railroads and
made monumental fortunes for themselves.

As a fascinated boy, Wayne could not then distinguish between what was possible in the America his father described and
what was likely for a young man from a family of eight without
a reasonable education. Wayne's father's legacy was, in a sense,
a litany of his own broken dreams—a subtle way of trying to
assuage the guilt of his own marginal performance by convincing
the kids that hope was alive and well in America.

So, long after Wayne reached his young manhood, he still
believed. His wartime experiences reinforced these notions
about boldness, audacity, and courage under fire. Yet after the
war, we are moved to speculate as to why Wayne continued to
carry these intense feelings with him, despite 6 long years of
living on the bare fringes of survival. Because his beliefs proved
hearty? Perhaps. More likely because his beliefs were so portable.
He could dream his dreams in sleazy hotels, in beat-up cars on
dirt roads. He could carry his faith in a beat-up suitcase, exercise
it by reading the ads for self-improvement courses in comic
books. He knew, he just knew, so it had to be so.

Each subsequent event in Wayne's life only served to fuel
the blazing faith in a great and generous Uncle in red, white, and
blue. Everything important that happened bore out the self-
fulfilling prophecy instilled during his childhood by his father.
His job at the Owl's Nest, the retirement of Leary, the night of

the flood, all of it suggesting to cynics a 1933 Warner Brothers Depression movie, drove Wayne harder up the slippery, glass hill. His early indoctrination had prepared him to meet his "luck" with a proper amount of "pluck."

There is a correlation with this, another peculiarly American business tendancy, which is a frenzied propensity to abuse a good thing to death. If one toy company invents a Frisbee, then there are fifty Frisbees to choose from within weeks. If one late-night TV talk show succeeds, then we soon have five vying for our attention.

If roast beef sandwiches can sate a big public hunger, then you can bet roast beef sandwiches will be served by Chinese restaurants in weeks. That's not simply saying that business thrives by copying a good thing; nor does it attempt to suggest that one firm own one product and that everyone else be restrained from selling a similar one. But it does remind us that the tendency to believe that you can do it just because somebody else has done it has produced some pretty notable failures in small business.

Wayne was done in by this kind of philosophical overreach. It obliterated his inherent talents and good business mind. Wayne simply pursued what he divined to be his destiny, a preordained mission to prove a man could still make it in America the honest old-fashioned way. We offer these humble thoughts to anyone who may have excessive confidence in those kinds of notions:

1] Had he remained with his original three locations, it is safe to venture the guess that Wayne would have become immensely wealthy, and deservedly so. So if you, or someone you know, or someone you work for has a little of Wayne Evans in him, try to short-cut the delusions early. It is not necessarily true that a little of a good thing can become, with luck and hard work, a lot of a good thing.

2] People in good, thriving businesses with an excess of real George F. Babbitt get-up-and-go would be well advised to channel some of that energy into good works for their fellow citizens. That may seem like wishful thinking, but never before has our country needed its energetic men more. That's how potholes get fixed and school budgets passed, and more police put on the beat and garbage gets cleaned up, and kids get a chance to enjoy organized sports. You look one of these days across the sandlots and playing fields of America. See who these men are who tirelessly, for whatever motives, are pouring their hearts and spirits into the bitter, frustrating, and often debilitating task of working with kids in sports. They are hardly ever relentless pursuers of the American Dream. On the contrary, most of them have gladly given up the luck and pluck business to devote their time. Vicarious? Sure, but so is the pursuit of unlimited riches.

It is, of course, blatantly naive to expect that anyone with a growing, healthy business can divert his pulsating drive toward things called good works or causes or movements. It is also equally naive, however, to think that the relentless pursuit of bigness for its own sake will make you any happier than you already are.

3] If you are one of those lucky ones whose business does lend itself to metered but quick expansion, then you must be prepared before the fact. Its been my experience that expanding horizons, when subjected to a "pay as you go" analysis, can eliminate nine-tenths of the possible failures. Thinking clearly is the best antidote for chronic overreach. By this, I don't mean careful budgeting and detailed planning. That's assumed. What I do mean is, what is the price of success you personally will pay? Longer hours? More traveling, less time for home and family? Less time for yourself? Who's it all for anyway?

Who?

4

Going Public—The Grand Illusion

H O W M A N Y men have been tempted to expose the meaty necks of their robust, growing enterprises to the tiny cluster of vampires who inhabit the shadowy edge of underworld Wall Street? Too many. Because out there among the tall towers of financial rectitude, they're waiting for greedy guys like you with greedier wives to be pushed into flushing years of grueling labor down the bowl. Going public to solve an inadequacy in your business is as idiotic as not going public when your company needs capital, and you and your bank agree your company is sufficiently mature to invite public money in.

More businesses go public for wrong reasons than right ones. A public issue of stock is too convenient a way to wallpaper over the cracks in the corporate walls. Companies which decide to make products they know little about often turn to public stock issues to legitimatize their pretensions (there's always a guy with a way around Polaroid's patents). Public money is frequently used to liquidate oppressive corporate debt by consolidation of that debt into a stock issue. This is surely a legitimate ploy, but it's too often abused; it's often used to cover up sloppy financial housekeeping. It's not coincidental that too many times the public learns too late that it was the dupe of a company management that simply couldn't live within its means. A company that will piss away private money, will tend to piss away bank money, and such a company will have a howling bacchanal with public money. And where's the businessman who can resist a party?

Take the money and run sounds like fun, just like wintering in Cap d'Antibes. Everyone talks about it—but—the only guys who can do it are the handful who really do winter in Cap d'Antibes. There are far more businessmen struggling to squeeze out 10 days in Miami Beach. Yet the lemmings fall into the sea—headlong, every day. There's always the chance of lucking out.

Act I

Cal Shaddon believed.

During the late Fifties, Cal and his partner, Jason, both engineering school graduates who abhorred engineering, decided that the rosy future lay in computers. They enrolled in programming school with the notion that they'd make piles of dough translating the then obscure, new sign language to businessmen too tired or too busy to comprehend the insolent machines. They would sell the idea that the machines could solve the problems businessmen themselves should have solved years before working with meager human beings, paper, and pencils.

Beginning in the *de rigeur,* dimly lit, downtown Manhattan loft, Cal and Jason began a data processing service bureau. Each morning, they'd pick up paper work from a few clients, dash to a key punching service to have the data prepared for the computer, rush the cards to a computer technology school where they rented a precious hour each day on the machine to process their client's information. They worked 16 hours a day. They managed to scrape out a marginal living.

Those days, in the late Fifties, were times when lots of bright young men had similar ideas. Two-desk service bureaus had popped up all over Manhattan like wild dandelions. By regularly combing through the trade press, the boys soon familiarized themselves with much of the Byzantine jargon of computer technology so they could display fancy footwork before the head-scratching, cigar-chomping grabbag of small clients they'd cultivated.

Aided by a reasonably sweet manner and a placid, wholesome personal appearance, Cal sold a few of his key punching customers the idea of programming entire operating procedures to save them time and money. They collected some nice fees in the process. The programs designed rarely worked well—as few

programs could which were designed for giant corporations and
adapted to small businesses. This small success stirred ego and
not unlike the corner retailer who calls himself a chain if he opens
a second store a mile up the road, the boys now renamed their
humble three-desk loft TRANSCONTINENTAL DATA SYSTEMS LIMITED
and replaced their answering service with a breathing, $85-a-
week secretary.

During these nascent days, a South Seas bubble was being
conjured on Wall Street. A few miles from their littered loft, a
maddened public was rushing insanely into the stock market each
day, gobbling up thousands upon thousands of new issue shares
of any company with the word "computer" somewhere in its
name. Cal learned of this mass hysteria on the long, mournfully
lonely, evening rides home on the Long Island Railroad. As a
defense against falling asleep and missing his stop, Cal began
picking up crumpled *Wall Street Journals* from the deserted commuter car seats and casually following the gyrations of computer
stocks. He even bought a few. In one case, he knew the company
and the men behind it. He giggled to Jason one day that the
owners of the particular company knew less than they did. Was
it not therefore inconceivable, he mused, that someday they'd lay
aside this filthy loft and take a joy ride on the market too? Hard-
headed but aware of the public's growing enchantment with computer stocks spurred by the growth of IBM, Jason suggested they
might chat with his brother-in-law who knew somebody who
knew somebody who knew somebody, who knew a marginal underwriter.

One Sunday afternoon on the 15-foot cement patio of Jason's modest little tract cottage on Long Island, he, Cal, and his
brother-in-law met with Kenneth Procter, the man at the other
end of all the "who knew somebodies." Procter was a securities
salesman who made a handsome living peddling computer stocks
to bored housewives and middle-class widows. He inevitably
rode lots of new issues into high flyers and possessed an endless
supply of new issue blocks in computer stocks to feed his growing
army of naifs. Yet for someone essentially no more than a customer's man, Procter's advice was sound. He told the boys that
the public would gobble anything that smelled of computers, but
insisted that they not rush things but borrow money first to

finance their expansion so that by year's end they could show reasonable six-figure sales. At the time of the meeting, they were grossing about $150,000 a year in total sales. He promised to take them to someone who would "position" them to go public when they were ready. In exchange for his services, he would take a block of shares for himself. It sounded incredible. Was Proctor kidding?

Then again, the thought of borrowing bank money by securing second mortages on their homes, borrowing from relatives, hiring salespeople, and opening larger offices at first terrified the boys. But the heady joy gas that was wafting around New York in those days hadn't deadened their faculties. They began to smell blood. Sheepishly, they solicited friends and relatives and were shocked by the ease with which they were able to extract five- and ten-thousand dollar loans. To their still greater shock, the officers at the bank were willing listeners. It was now 1964. Money was cheap and easy at banks. The Johnson economy was starting to balloon. Incredulously, Cal and Jason walked out of the bank two months later with a commitment for $50,000.

They now set the money to work. Having neither the experience nor the innate business skills necessary to build an enterprise from within, Cal and Jason turned to the clumsy trial-and-error method of taking programmers, salespeople, and administrative personnel from competitors.

On the surface, the process seemed to work. Sales volume inched up. The quality of output worsened steadily, but in those days, that was no reason for hampering sales.

Early in the game, the boys had learned the copout against which there was no defense; computers don't make errors, people do. Few clients could challenge such sophistry. All they knew was that their own people said one thing and the outside bureaus who processed the data said another. The resultant confusion enabled the boys to bluff their way through a difficult period when chronic quality control problems might have stopped them dead in their tracks in another industry.

It was now 1965. The Vietnam escalation had brought a bloody rose to the cheek of the U.S. economy. It was now time, Procter reasoned, for the boys to make the assault on Wall Street. A phalanx of blue-suited lawyers and accountants was assembled, properly credentialized and given a simple brief to get TDS "going."

Sales volume was up to $400,000 for fiscal 1965. A pretax profit of about $21,000 was anticipated. It was enough. The rest was easy. Even as they wrote the prospectus, prices of new computer stocks were rising like the temperature at Delhi at high noon. The eager little band pressed forward. So great was the demand for computer stocks that it didn't take more than 2 months for them to find a reasonably solvent underwriter with capital enough to bring TDS public.

The stock was capitalized at $750,000 of which 40% was offered to the public ($300,000 worth). After underwriting costs, legal and accounting fees, the TDS boys were in possession of about $200,000 in hard cash. The stock opened at 3 over the counter and closed its first day of trading at 5½. In 1965, TDS earned just $15,000 after taxes. Cal and Jason had never earned more than $18,000 each in their best year. One's imagination is not hard-pressed to visualize the scene at the loft that first trading day when the boys calculated the value of their own 250,000 shares at 5½. *(Curtain)*

Having legitimately extracted $200,000 from a greedy public, TDS now sought intelligent means of using it. At that point, the best conceivable advice would have been to dump the whole lump into one velvety, green bag and invest it in real estate. They then could have settled into their new plush leather armchairs and clinked glasses of Dom Perignon over a sumptuous repast of caviar and Cornish hen. But they made the fatal and inevitable error of all newly minted public companies run by newly inflated egos. They began at once to think big.

At this point in our narrative, it will be helpful to break in with a simple warning. If you do go public, or a friend of yours does, or the local pizzeria whose sausage pizza you love does, remember to track down a copy of an ad run in national magazines during the early Sixties by the Volkswagen people. It was written by a genius. But don't read it to study brilliant advertising copy, read it to learn about survival. The ad's headline reads "Think Small." The copy soberly invites your instincts to consider the virtues of smallness, of simplicity of design, of fewer working parts, of convenience, of ease of parking, of fuel economy—of all those things the big chrome giants from Detroit were not.

The idea of thinking small was disarmingly basic. It pinpointed a social revolution before the men who study these phenomena in great universities did. It challenged the basic article of faith which had propelled American business since the time of the robber barons: Big was good.

To a new public company, it teaches that merely expanding scale and scope of an enterprise does not automatically ensure its success. The raw nerve of growth is often malignant as our heroes were soon to learn. So rip out the ad, frame it, and hang it over anyone's head who's apt to think his newly public company will be challenging the big, bad guys of the Big Board in a shootout for market share. Hang the ad in the board room and consider the ultimate irony of it all; even Volkswagen didn't heed its own good, sensible ads. Detroit finally learned to think small with Pintos and Vegas and Gremlins. Volkswagen's response was to build bigger VW's. Our Japanese friends watched with characteristic care. They thought small too. And look w`.at happened. Someone in Tokyo saw that ad too.

Act II

As in a classic Greek drama, our story unfolds with the entrance of a new personage or presence which will move the principal characters into previously uncharted emotional seas. In the case of our heroes, it was a disease. We'll call it Acquisitionosis. Its prime symptom is rapacity, caused by the rudimentary metabolism of public issue.

TDS went public for 40% of its restructured net worth, leaving 60% of its equity in the hands of our heroes, the founding partners, and their growing phalanx of lawyers, underwriters, accountants, and key employees. This remaining equity presented a tantalizing opportunity to buy other small companies, public or private, for that marvelously appropriate currency called "paper."

TDS basically had no business other than its operations as a computer service bureau. Its rise to status as a public company changed nothing. It was still two guys who rented time on someone else's computer puffed into stock certificates and shot into the wilds of the over-the-counter market. By long hours and application, there was little doubt TDS could support our two magnates in reasonable middle-class style, but there was much doubt about the company's capacity to do anything else. To their credit, a few of the initial investors made a fast few bucks and ran like hell.

The boys, however, charged with steering this now great vessel across the shoals of corporate America, seized upon an idea. The opportunity to grow must come by grafting other companies. The means would be its stock. Continuing acquisitions would keep the price of the stock pumped high and this, in turn, would increase the value of the stock as a bargaining counter against potential acquisitionees. Enough time, enough buyouts, and enough public relations could pump the stock high enough to justify a secondary offering a year or so later, then the inevitable dump of inside stock. All very common. All very legal. And all very 1960's.

TDS reasoned that more dough could be made faster by acquiring small companies with their paper, barraging the Street with publicity, moving the stock upward on rumor, and dumping later than by what appeared to be the tortuous, complex, tangled route of the straight line—actually using the golden time and money bought to build a bona fide business that could have a reasonable chance to make some real money.

So Cal and Jason fanned out across the Northeast, seaching for tiny gem companies in related fields owned by men naive enough to exchange the fruits of a lifetime's work for a two-dollar ticket on a longshot. They had few takers. Not because the owners were any less glib or romantic about their companies' futures with potential merger partners than they were in their prospectus, but because of the naked irony that acquisitionosis was an epidemic. "Who the hell needs you?" one midget electronics baron replied, "I can do the same thing, and what's more, I will."

Harvey, the company's P.R. man, started to sweat. He began getting nervous for news. The stock was beginning to sag, at round 4.

After 6 months as a public company, TDS moved to slick new quarters, hired ten new people who sat around much of the time aimlessly discussing "projects," wondering what to do and taking each other to lunch in fancy restuarants on company credit cards, struggling to find ways of stretching 3 hours' work into 10. Desperation now set into Harvey's state of mind. He confessed his growing despair to Jason. Jason thought things out and finally had a blinding flash of brilliance. Where would they be most likely to uncover small entrepreneurs most susceptible to their blandishments? In the sturdy technical minds of pocket-sized, New England components manufacturers? In the wildly greedy crannies of Long Island's electronics row along the great Expressway? Never. The answer was obvious. In the equally fatuous dreams of other small software computer bureaus in Manhattan? Of course. In New York City at that time, there were literally dozens upon dozens of tiny data service bureaus owned by floundering fools two years out of IBM Training School. They owned a loft, a few customers, and not much more. After all, Jason concluded, TDS paper was better than toilet paper. Bingo!

They began acquiring scrubby little data processing bureaus and with them, more customers, more overheads, and little or no profits. Thousands of shares of TDS and, in some cases, chunks of hard cash thus blew into the wind. The balloon began acquiring some air. The company's stained walnut conference table was thrown out and replaced with a $4,500 rosewood, decorator original to accommodate the burgeoning Board of Directors meetings.

Thursday evenings, 20 grown men sat around that rosewood table speaking in hushed, solemn voices. TDS, hardly out of the loft, was now a miniconglomerate. Ambition had drawn them together. They had an appointment with a destiny none of them yet conceived. To what unknown glories would their grand scheme now take them? Self-congratulation and the pretentious disease of ego infested their collective minds as they puffed expensive cigars.

But Harvey the public relations man was less sanguine. He'd been down this road before. He continued nervously pondering about his client's future. The continuing march of small acquisitions was fine, he figured, but what the stock really hungered after was a gigantic contrivance, something which would appeal to a slowly souring public appetite.

He telephoned Cal and Jason one morning. He told Cal that

he wasn't the only insider worried. He confided that George, the company lawyer, and Alex, the company's accountant, had expressed deep concern too. They were under relentless pressure from Winton, the dour underwriter and board member, who was starting to cavil aloud about the wisdom of his firm's continued support of TDS stock at 3 1/2.

Harvey taxied to TDS's spiffy new headquarters and confronted the boys. He was precise and direct. If they couldn't get something exciting afoot by year's end, Winton would take a powder; without the support of Winton's brokerage firm at 3 1/2, the stock would crumble completely. Winton had been getting heat from his senior partners. With so many crummy computer stocks rising each day, how come their crummy computer stock wallowed well below 5? Was there no R&D breakthrough to announce? No new joint venture? No licensing agreements with Xerox? No dramatic earnings increases? What the hell were these two bums doing with the money anyway? Cal uneasily lifted his arms off the $4,500 rosewood decorator table as Harvey relentlessly droned out Winton's vocal misgivings. Cal and Jason looked at each other. They were both sweating hard. Had they scant time to plan for growth before, it now appeared they had none.

A week of frenetic brainstorming ensued. That Friday, Cal and Jason, exhausted by the process, shuffled together across a dark Manhattan street toward Penn Station to a late commuter train.

Suddenly a face popped up from among the wearied commuters in wrinkled suits. It was an old college buddy of Cal's, and after a tentative exchange of glances, the face wrinkled into a smile and the men shook hands. It was Henry Jenks, soon to be a major protagonist in the unfolding drama.

The three men had about an hour's wait for a train that time of night. They went to a quiet commuter bar for a few drinks mixed with a few memories. They exchanged fraternity stories for twenty minutes or so, and then, Henry veered off into a grumbling tale of woe about his boss.

Henry worked as head merchandiser for a paranoid mail order magnate whose carnival shlockhouse sales techniques had made him a rich man during the late Fifties. As vigorous competition arrived, however, he refused to streamline his antiquated order processing methods. This resulted in lost orders, delayed shipments, confused procedures, and increasingly plunging sales. Henry said he'd repeatedly pleaded with his boss to make changes, but the old man, a typical Incarnation Fallacy entrepreneur, wouldn't budge. Henry's misery deepened. He was looking to get out. Did the boys know anyone in the mail order business? Then, rising to meet his train, Henry sighed, and as if Zeus had commanded each word to roll forth from his mouth on cue, he said, "I'd show a guy how to make money today. You do it with computers, like you guys. Program it, bring it into the 1960's, and sell like mad. That's what I'd do if I had a person to work with. This guy's a hopeless egomaniac."

"Henry," Cal squealed. "Sit down. You'll catch the next train."

Henry sat down. What then unfolded was pure Sam Goldwyn, 1943. They remained in the bar until midnight when they were thrown out half-drunk with triumph. They staggered eastward cross town to a cheap hotel where they rented a shabby room. Then like Gene Kelly, Sidney Miller, and Dan Dailey, the three commuters hammered out a master plan that would make them all rich and TDS would go off into the Sunset kissing the Chairman of the New York Stock Exchange. *(Fade Out.)*

Before we raise the curtain on Act III, let's examine for a moment or two, the chilly realities of the mail order business. First, they are among the most frequent failures in small business venturing. Their fatality rate, no doubt, is related to the huge numbers of amateurs who embark on it thinking it an effortless route to millions in one's spare time without quitting the regular job.

In practice, the mail order business is as professional and precise a science as you can get. Its no place for dreamers. The mail order battlefield is littered with the corporate arms and legs of some of this country's leading companies, who have stepped lightly into this booby-trapped province. Despite this, amateurs continue to dive in because the mechanics of mail order selling are so damn tantalizing that it is all too simple to hypnotize oneself into thinking of easy success. This is a game for tough pros.

Had Cal and Jason been a little smarter and a little less

human, Act III of our drama might never have happened. But their insistence on diving into the icy waters, knowing beforehand where all the sharks lay, testifies not only to their now hopelessly bloated egos, but to their unvarnished desperation. They had forgotten that less than a year before, they were two IBM training school dropouts, struggling to make $15,000 a year selling time on a computer. They were now hotshot corporate men. So anything was possible.

What were these tempting sirens calling from the mail order shores?

Index finger on pinky, Henry began:

First, fellas, in mail order selling, you get paid by the consumer *before* you pay your supplier for your inventory.

Second, boys, you need no salesmen. Newspapers, magazines, catalogs don't eat, don't have mortgages, and don't support families.

Third, lads, you can buy an item to sell by mail for about a third or even less its retail value, advertise it in good national media at an efficient cost of under another third the retail value, and make a full third profit for the house. Not bad.

Fourth, gentlemen, you don't even need a store from which to pitch your wares. So you can sell merchandise competitively to retail stores without paying rent.

Fifth, my good men, this is the mid-Sixties; inflation and boom are rampaging through the nation. Retail stores are having nervous breakdowns. They can't get good help. Consumers are getting angrier and millions are beginning to buy stuff by mail they've never dreamed of buying by mail before.

Sixth, the consumer balloon has thrust upward a whole new class of consumers earning between $12,000 and $17,000 a year who were full-fledged, credit card carrying buyers. They prefer to buy by mail and pay later, and the small businessman likes to buy a mail order item, charge it to his company credit card, and write it off, even though he uses it personally or gives it to his wife.

Neat. Right? All the business needed was organization, Henry said. Orders picked and processed the old way took too long to handle and frustrated the hell out of consumers. The quality of mailing lists were being debased and milked dry by too many direct mail merchandisers. All these woes could be solved, he concluded, by the application of a totally computerized operation. This vast panorama dramatically painted by Henry brought Cal and Jason to their knocking knees. Why, it was all so easy. It was so simple. Cal and Jason's juices began pumping. That night, they told Henry to quit his job. They told him to hole up at home and emerge with a workable plan to get TDS into the general merchandise mail order business in quick order. They wanted a plan with big numbers that they could submit to their board at the first annual meeting the following week.

Act III

Henry dashed home and set immediately to work. He drafted a plan to duplicate his present employer's business in record time. He rationalized, with some justification, that the old mountebank deserved a good kick in the ass anyway. Meanwhile, the salivating partners at TDS undertook to check out Henry. They were immensely pleased with the intelligence. Henry was reputed as honest, slightly neurotic, adept, reasonably talented, and one of the best hard-nosed professionals in the field. His record of successes was strong and his blistering critique of his employer checked out as well. He had not lied or exaggerated. Honesty was an increasingly rare quality in their milieu, so the boys got to feeling they'd scored a real coup in locating Henry and tapping him for the idea on computerized mail order selling.

After several preliminary meetings, Henry dramatically presented his final plan. It was four paragraphs long:

1] Henry Jenks' record needs no elaboration. He sold $100,000,000 worth of mail order merchandise during his 15 years in the business.

2] If he had a sound computerized processing system to back up his merchandising skills, he could outsell his present company two to one and could easily produce $4,000,000 in sales within 2 years. He felt perfectly secure forecasting no less than four percent after taxes. To do this job, he wanted $50,000 a year plus all the fringes.

3]   He needed $150,000 to start up a new TDS division.
4]   What were they waiting for?

TDS bit. Perhaps it is fairer to say they bought. Henry's plan was illustrated and charted by one of the best graphics houses in town. It was presented to the TDS board. Everyone endorsed the plan on the spot. Winton took the presentation to his partners who liked it too. Finally, the heat was beginning to ease. Cal and Jason's frequency of trips to the bathroom slumped.

The official debut of the new Mr. Henry Mail Village was announced to the financial world. Shortly thereafter, full-page ads in credit card subscriber magazines, metropolitan daily and Sunday papers, and Sunday supplements began to appear pushing mustache cups, cheap luggage, "Fool 'Em Fast False Fannies," and similar commodities. This was followed by military surplus tents, combat boots, tool kits, shoes, Americana Patchwork Quilts made in Singapore, kegs of nails and brass spittoons. At Christmastime, Mail Village published a 64-page, color catalog and mailed it to a finely selected set of lists reaching over 1,000,000 consumers.

The catalog pulled business. Sales of the Mr. Henry Mail Village Division spilled over into $1,000,000 within 4 months of its birth. Henry had delivered. But his estimates were off. Start-up expenses originally estimated about $150,000 now ran over $250,000 for the first full year so no significant profits were shown.

The TDS annual report, over four months late, owing to the company's absolute need to include the mail order volume in the sales figures (many expenses were thrown into the following year), showed the dramatic increase in sales the boys had hoped for. Yet the effects of these apparently good results were mild. The slide in the price of TDS shares had been arrested at around 3. Cal and Jason had merely bought breathing time.

But the boys were flushed with confidence. They decided that the future of TDS now lay in the application of computer sciences to mass merchandising mail order techniques. They acquired a company dealing in mailing lists and a roto printer. Finally, their corporate ego inflated to the bursting point: They went "International."

They decided that Europe was a vast wasteland of mail

order potential. With their typical naïveté, of all countries in which to begin a computerized mail order operation, they selected France. In spite of the French proclivity to skepticism and suspicion of merchants with less than 400 years in a neighborhood, TDS opened a Paris branch. It was a joint operation with a French company run by the shiftless son of a provincial cookie manufacturer.

The French operation was comprised of a secretary who spent her days waiting for a phone call from her boy friend who was chasing her cousin around Nice and a salesman who tramped up and down the streets of Paris trying to flush out mail order firms in need of computer expertise.

Cal took several trips to "check out" the French operation. Part of that process was repeated trips to famous couture houses by Cal's wife, exquisite dinners at the Tour D'Argent discussing business with his worthless French partner, and a few trips to the Loire Valley during which Cal acquired some excellent wines. One evening in Paris, Cal was summoned to take a call from New York. It was Jason. He babbled and screamed and, finally, choked out his story. The jig was up.

It seemed the latest Mr. Henry Mail Village catalog had bombed so miserably that it was unlikely that one-fifth the costs of mailing and printing would be recovered. The key board member, Winton, had resigned in disgust. His firm would now abandon TDS stock to the slag heap. Cal staggered out of the phone booth thunderstruck. It was Get-Your-Ass-Home time.

People had started muttering about a recession in late 1969. Aerospace jobs disappeared, executives, engineers, and waiters were being laid off. Suddenly, one could get seated in certain previously mobbed restaurants. But a recession? Surely, that was a 1950's word that merely meant that Lockheed had knocked off a few more engineers 3,000 miles away. Neither Cal nor Jason had ever thought that the thing they read about in *The New York Times* would ever reach them.

It burst upon the chancey fortunes of TDS like the leveling of a city by an atomic weapon. The catalog that bombed shook all the assumptions the boys had about mail merchandising, about computers, about the possibilities of getting by on sheer balls during the 1960's.

When Cal arrived home, he confronted a gravely concerned

Henry. He wasn't so shocked at the disasterous showing of the latest catalog as he was concerned about the high inventories he'd laid away in anticipation of a booming year. They would have to get busy slashing prices or face a liquidity crisis.

With Winton's firm no longer behind the stock, with the big bust on the stock market just ahead, Cal and Jason began a sell-off of inventory, keeping one step ahead of the bank just to draw salaries. Their computer business, which had been slowly dying, now commenced the death rattle.

By early 1971, TDS stock dropped below $1 and was all but delisted. Weakening mail order sales now carried most of the company's volume.

Software projects and data processing income plunged below the levels prior to the stock issue. The shiny, new computer, installed in the heady afterglow of success just 2 years before, stood in dreary silence much of the day bearing mute testimony to the folly of small-time ego. "Everytime I pass that sonofabitch machine," Cal once said, "I feel it grinning at me, eating away at my bones."

TDS doggedly pressed the battle for survival in mail order alone. But another poison-dipped dart was now shot into the hapless little company: competition. Their early success in selling gimmicks and general utility household goods by mail was not unique. There's no patent on a good idea. When Henry talked to Cal and Jason that humid night at Penn Station, there was another man named Stanley who talked the same way to a banker who lent him the money to begin a business to compete with TDS.

And so, the ultimate small business irony. The knockoff artist is knocked off. And that's just what happened. The Stanley of this story was an advertising man who made no pretensions about computerizing or internationalizing or $4,500 rosewood conference tables. He worked out of a loft. He bought low and sold high. He squirreled his profits and plowed them back in the business. He began small, tested, probed, and expanded very slowly. His efforts paid off and his business obtruded into TDS's by offering similar goods at lower prices. He didn't have Paris branches to support.

Between the pasting Stanley was giving them and the recession, Cal and Jason dove for the trenches and took cover.

They cut personnel; they spun off division after division. They sublet part of their quarters, closed down the international division, and crossed their fingers. But now they were cornered quarry. If they only had a little more time—time to look for a new field, something exciting, something to jazz up the stock—something. Anything.

Each new mail order venture now further instilled the notion that their grand design was a crown of thorns. Abandoned by their Svengalis, begirt by sneering board members, shrugged at by unyielding bankers, hopelessly baffled by the unflustered suicidal promotions of Henry, Cal and Jason ran out of breath. TDS published loss after loss each quarter. Finally, the merciful deed was done in late February of 1972. The bank called in their notes. Cal and Jason sold their inventory and trademarks to Stanley, closed the door, paid what they could, and left. The two young eagles of two years before were now old plucked chickens.

AUTOPSY

It doesn't require a brilliant pathologist to guess how the business died. Ego, greed, and a rapacious naïveté killed TDS as they will kill any business whose growth is prematurely mutated by going public before its time. Not easy to see, however, are the subterranean dynamics, the forces which speed the death of a preemie public company by maneuvering it around hairpin turns at high speed toward the inexorable end. Have a good look at them. Someday, you may meet them.

1. THE *"Keep the Stock Price Up"* FORCE

If you go public, you will rapidly be the victim of a conspiracy to drive you crazy, bankrupt, or both. This deadly force is never cloaked in a menacing hood or black robe. It is most often an advancing army led by your investment banker, your key men, your well meaning P.R. man, your friends and relatives, the boys at the club. The general of this army is probably your wife. It is she who leads the circle of vultures around the carcass of your formerly private company, urging you to keep the air pumping through the corpse by acquiring new companies, new processess, secret patents—anything that will push up the stock price and increase your paper net worth. These well-meaning, loving people will hammer away at you day and night. They will repeat phrases like "run like a thief, cash your chips at the high, issue a secondary, make a statement" until you're ready to scream. They mean well. They want you to be rich.

These forces are subtle. They can't be isolated and easily identified like so many other virus strains. That's because they're so easy to believe. After all, why the hell did you go public if not to pull out your dough? It takes steel nerve to withstand that kind of logical assault on your perfectly human acquisitive impulses. So you can slowly get drawn in. After a while, you'll do anything that holds the faintest promise of moving the price of the stock.

And there's no release from this trap in a bad market, either. People will merely tell you that this insane thing must be done because the stock must at least nose-dive at the same rate as the competition's. In a rising market, they'll make you feel like a tortoise racing a Ferrari. In a bad market, you've got to act like Churchill holding off the *Luftwaffe*. You must face this pressure and take a stand.

First, tell everyone to shut up. Tell them to stop worrying about the price of the shares and start helping you run the business so that you can make more money, show bigger earnings, and hope the stock will eventually rise on performance.

Second, make believe you didn't go public at all. Fire the worthless bums you wanted to fire. Talk to your banker about financing as if he still remains the most important guy in your life. Don't start diversifying until you are absolutely convinced you are doing as much as you can do in your own field with the money you've raised.

2.   THE *"We Can Do Anything"* FORCE

Look into the mirror. Grit your teeth a little. Its tough to admit for a big, important guy like you heading a newly minted public company with a few hundred real live stockholders, a dozing board of directors, and a mysterious trading symbol, you are still what is commonly known as a "cocker." If you run a small business you have a small-business mentality. You may think big, but the truth is, if you had to manipulate the hundreds of millions of dollars, the people, the intricate financings, the plants, the movements of billions of tons of raw materials of a big corporation, you'd probably have a stroke every day. That kind of stuff can only be done by a phalanx of corporate men who manipulate these things as symbols. You work with reality. So you shouldn't think you're building a dam in the Congo when you're calling the plumber to fix a leak in the ladies room on the first floor.

This admittedly disappointing resignation to reality will provide immeasurable insight into dealing with the "We Can Do Anything" disease when it hits your company. It begins reasonably enough. Small companies pride themselves on flexibility and rapid response to market trends. This fact often makes some of them scornful of the large corporations whose ponderous, slowly grinding, bureaucratic processes seem to leave them behind in competitive battles. The big guys may lose a few battles, to be sure. But they hardly ever lose a war. That's the difference between big guys and little guys.

Big guys can recover from even the most appalling screw-ups imaginable with asset stripping, management changes, mergers, acquisitions, and financial leverage. If the cost of the Edsel fiasco was the price Ford eventually paid for the Mustang triumph, Ford could afford to pay it over again and still survive handsomely. You couldn't.

As responsive and bright as your management team may be, unleashing them into fields remotely related to yours is the classic suicide impulse of the small-business mentality. You could, of course, recruit outside brains. But that can be worse. Outsiders don't know the dynamics of your company. Coming in when you've just gone public worsens their confusion. They don't know who holds the keys to which toilets. They are anxious to please. They always appear to possess the formula for some potent elixir for new profits in an esoteric field you know nothing about.

Going public prematurely invites the tempting notion that you can now do anything you want. That damn grass is always greener no matter how you try to stay in your own yard. So our heroes in computer software find themselves selling copper spittoons in Sunday newspaper supplements. If it was a good idea after the fact of going public, why wasn't it a good idea before? The truth is that it would have been a bad idea either way. But public money served not as the vehicle but the excuse to do something dumb. And that is what the small-business mentality is about. When it's your dough, you watch it like a baby. When it's something loosely called "public money" or, more aptly, "Wall Street Welfare," sheer insanity takes over.

3. THE FORCE OF *"Grandeur"*

When business is private, it can do what it likes. When it goes public, it has to please a new public. A band of stockholders, a board, brokers, investment men and public agencies surround the new company with a sense of public responsibility that is entirely just. But some guys don't know when to stop.

Too often, the pompous distortions of public posture result in vacuous posturing and ego-tripping. The whole idea of performance for the shareholders becomes a shabby charade. Genuine corporate prestige is built on dignity, humanity, sweat, know-how, and staying power under fire. Suddenly becoming a public company is not an excuse to begin acting like an ass.

These three forces we've recounted all hammered TDS into an early grave. Within the seeds of their public issue were the potentials for achievement too. Why did our two heroes act like such dummies? Are we being unfair? Perhaps. But let's advance a few ideas as to what they might have done, in the hope that the next guys might have a chance to succeed.

TDS might have tried to use the time and money bought by the public issue to look for a corner of the small-time computer business in which they could specialize. It doesn't seem at all improbable that these two intelligent, energetic young men might have found an untilled field to plow. It made terribly good sense at the time to continue pushing forward in computers, a line where they would have been more likely to shine.

The boys seemed seized by a knowing fear that, newly born, they were about to die—like the twilight of a mayfly. They lacked the central, essential faith in what they were doing prior to going public, to continue it after they went public. They were so busy pinching themselves, they simply couldn't think. The route to survival they saw was a detour, not a direct route. They sensed the bloom was on the rose in computer stocks. And it was. It further seems appropriate to suggest that it is they who might well have sought to be absorbed by a larger, stronger computer sciences company, rather than puffing up balloons of their own.

If there was a crying need for computer services in the mail order field, they should have serviced that need. They should have developed programs to meet the needs of the successful mail order firms and thus profited from them without the risk of going into the business itself. But they aspired to big things. In their headlong rush to build volume, to find prestige and status, to promote their stock, they didn't have time to manage their business or hire the right personnel to do it. They predictably picked seasoned bureaucrats and well-credentialed *apparachnicks*. With less frenzy and perhaps a heightened sensitivity to the genuine needs of their business, the boys could well have attracted bright computer men who, in time, might have opened new paths of growth for the company, which it could have traveled with relative ease. We'll never know. Business life is so often a choice between perils.

5

The Incarnation Fallacy

IN 1651, Louis XIV, who wasn't exactly a corner candy store operator when it came to managing political business, summarized his attitudes toward his enterprise (seventeenth century France) with a phrase of monumental conceit, "L'état c'est moi." (I am the state). A few centuries later, his spiritual and temporal successor, Charles de Gaulle, no less modest but perhaps a scant more discreet, said, "When I spoke at Algiers [during the fateful days of the 1958 crisis] everyone understood that this time it was France who was speaking."

This type of delusion is not confined to colossal figures of French history. American business is full of those who believe they are the business incarnate. Henry Ford thought he was the Ford Motor Company. Adolph Ochs was The New York Times Company. The ubiquitousness of William Randolph Hearst could be felt down to the last inflection of the most remote editorials in the small-town papers he published. Popular journalism has labeled these men tycoons or robber barons, but they were something considerably larger than moneymakers: They were true believers in the incarnation fallacy. The men who built these empires became so inextricably entwined with them that they were unable to distinguish between their handiwork and their own bodies. Every light bulb, every desk, every assembly line belt, every worker, every ad, and every line written by every clerk was as much a part of their self images as their fingernails, arms, or eyes. Try to tell them about the dozens of people who helped make the company. They'll never believe it.

Most people tend to accept the I.F. mentality passively as

long as it doesn't live in the mind of an incorrigible martinet. It's easy to recognize and rebel against a rotten egomaniac who is abusive and cruel to his staff, but the cheerful I.F. boss is quite another animal. He's often charming, seemingly benign, and at times, an out-and-out buffoon. He can court the love of his staff by a constant prattle of jokes, favors, gifts, and compliments. All he wants is for everyone to admit that he is the business and the business is him. So his benevolent despotism tricks his staff into complacency, and they fail to see the damage that he's doing to the business.

It's perfectly reasonable to assume that the gut instinct, ambition, greed, intellectual drive, and natural proclivity to moneymaking required to build a business must be accompanied by a heavy helping of unvarnished ego. Men who build mammoth enterprises are often spared the revelation of the absurdity of their Incarnation Fallacy mentality by retirement, death, infirmity, or replacement by heirs. When the head man's I.F. personality begins to take its toll on the company, however, the staff must be prepared to battle the chief executive to assure the company's survival.

In large corporations, a phalanx of bright, rugged executives with thick skins can generally protect an I.F. company founder from his own monster ego until the "King" decides to quit. Large organizations like this develop a sort of counterinsurgency guerrilla strength, which by sheer inertia often grows powerful enough to counterveil assaults on the corporate body by the willful inanities of the egomaniacal ruler. Little companies have no such defenses.

That's why, if you run or work for a small company, you've got to learn, early on, how to recognize the deadly danger signals of the I.F. mentality in your head man. If you do, you won't be as surprised over losing your job as you might have been had you continued to believe that the driving entrepreneur who heads your company was a genius, and not a clown whose pretentions to immortality are going to take you down with him.

HARRY FOUNDED his New York advertising agency in 1949 by running classified ads for marginal, struggling young electronics firms. His hope was to make enough money to expand into the larger world of consumer products advertising.

He went busted three times along the way, but managed, with the indispensable help of three dedicated associates, to withstand the tempests common to the advertising business. In 1954, his company lost a large account. It happened just after they had undertaken a crushingly expensive move from a loft on the west side of Manhattan to a posh new six-room suite on Madison Avenue. Harry was desolate but maintained his faith. He gritted his teeth and cut his salary by $50 a week (while his three trusted associates went with no pay at all for nearly 2 months). This unshakable faith paid off. New clients slowly drifted in, bringing prosperity, expansion, and, eventually, my friend Ben.

Ben arrived in 1956. Harry was already a legend in his time. He arrived at work every day in a Rolls Royce and ate a hearty bacon and eggs, kippers, and oatmeal English-style breakfast in his private Tudor dining room before taking the first calls of the day. He was waited on by a valet in white gloves who served his eggs from a heavy, sterling silver chafing dish and poured his coffee from an antique silver pot worth over $2,000. Harry sat alone, surrounded by the long shafts of early morning light pouring through the stately, leaded glass windows. He looked out those windows at a cluster of midtown skyscrapers, which stood in brooding silence as if waiting for him to stir or push the button to start the city. He turned the pages of *The New York Times,* the *Wall Street Journal,* and the New York *Daily News* (where he read his daily horoscope). After the servant cleared away the dishes, he slipped into his cavernous office and began pushing buzzers on his desk. And the agency, as if plugged into his index finger, suddenly electrified and sprang into life for the day.

Amid this regal splendor, tiptoed Harry's three old stalwarts (now minority shareholders in the company), spreading good words and cheerful encouragement, among the sympathetic ears of all the employees. Interspersed between their concerned nods were tales of Harry's early days, repeatedly amplified and distorted to instill a sense of "history," they said, in the minds of the younger employees.

Harry's I.F. mentality was dreadful but tolerable. Once a week, Harry would invite all department heads into his private

dining room for an epicurean luncheon feast catered by a celebrated French restaurant. The ostensible purpose of these elaborate luncheons was the generation of informal conversation on
weighty matters affecting the agency during that particular week.
But they also served to enhance the personal *Gemütlichkeit* Harry
had cultivated since he began in business. These luncheons became excuses for Harry to rise to great flights of fatuous oratory
before a captive audience. While his gleeful executives stuffed
themselves with saucisson and poached sea bass, Harry monopo-
lized the conversation. He narrated, over and over again, how he,
single-handedly, saved the Tru-Bloo girdle account by quickly
rushing to the offended client on a crippled two-engine Cessna
because all the regular airlines were socked in on bad weather.
Or he scribbled suggestions concerning every campaign in progress in the shop. Didn't so-and-so think the new beer commercial
would be substantially sounder if photographed with such-and-
such an acting technique rather than a thus-and-so acting technique?

Who would stand and challenge Harry? Where was a he-
man among these gutless wonders at the table gobbling Harry's
expensive food? Was old Harry's voice intimidating? Did he
boom it off the walls like a raving maniac? Were the memos that
followed the luncheons so biting, so vicious, and threatening?
Did they all sit in meek, silent approval of Harry's cracked stories,
dumb jokes, and inane advertising ideas?

According to Ben, Harry always spoke or wrote memos in
a civil, almost scholarly tone. He never shouted, rarely frowned.
He always suggested, never demanded; he nudged, never prod-
ded. So naturally, nobody ever demurred. Harry was a dream
boss.

The "silent majority" at the festive table were all well paid,
smug, reasonably competent professionals who had just polished
off a magnificent luncheon with their boss and whose judgment
of his nutty utterings was clouded by the mythology that now
lived in the walls of the agency. Harry wasn't always right, they
rationalized, but, by God, he had one helluva batting average.
Ben agreed. It was impossible for him to conceive of anything
else. He earned $40,000 a year. He had what could safely be
described as one of the most secure jobs on Madison Avenue.

Harry would never fire Ben. Everyone knew it. Especially Harry. Without Ben, three or four heavyweight accounts would flush down the drain. So Ben enjoyed working for Harry. He collected his 800 smackers a week. He unraveled a fast credit card anywhere he wanted, and he thought of Harry's egomania as something, at worst, rather amusing.

Ben giggled and snickered for the following ten years, blind to the reality that Harry's preoccupation with his own infallability was gravely impeding the growth of the company during an era when competitors were leaping ahead into the big dollar billings. Ben often asked Harry about what plans they should be making for the years ahead. Harry's reply was predictable. Harry never agonized about the future. Did he need to? When he was along, over there on the west side, in that crummy little rat's nest, did he ever worry about the future? Dammit man, he created the future! He didn't plan anything, he just went out and met the day, and one day at a time was the way he conquered the biggest accounts in the nation.

The "funny little man," as he was called in the agency, didn't bother anyone, but over the years, his egomania eroded the agency's chance of survival in the treacherous rapids of the 1960's advertising world.

Harry willfully refused to merge the copy and art departments into teams so that the good creative people could cross-fertilize. In the traditionally structured, outmoded atmosphere of Harry's agency, many of the brightest, most stable young men Ben had attracted to the agency resigned in disgust after brief exposure to Harry. (It can't be very soothing to Ben to consider that these young kids saw through Harry in months, while he never knew what hit him over a period of years.) Harry attributed the agency's high employee turnover to "those little snotnose bastards with ingrate mentalities." There were snotnoses everywhere in the agency business during the 1960's. But that was no reason to let talent flush down the drain without a fight.

While Harry rejected young talent with good ideas for innovation, he spurned the idea of retiring his two aging associates, even though their presence blocked the free flow of ideas and change, on all levels of the agency. Harry responded to criticism of the old employees by reminding the critic that "they chipped in to help pay the rent many a month when we were over on 42nd Street."

Martha was 68 and lived in a 1939, Rosalind Russell world. Her conception of the advertising business was of shoulder-padded, wisecracking women wearing snoods, draping themselves over massive oak desks, chucking frustrated Adolph Menjous under the chins, whispering dynamite ideas for the next Oompa Flakes campaign. Her professional standards were founded on the snappy, rat-ta-tat-tat department store retail style copy she had mastered during the Depression. She used expressions like "that youngster had a flair for writing" and still called layout men "sketch artists." But despite these arcane notions about the world of advertising, she was still Harry's first employee.

In those maddening young days, she not only wrote the copy, but typed the insertion orders, went out for coffee, mailed out the billing, dunned the slow accounts, kept the books, and often gave her not unattractive body for the survival of the stumbling young agency. Some people thought she had a secret crush on Harry all her life.

Martha's body was now flaccid and she couldn't give it anymore; her mind was like a sealed, cluttered old attic at whose door the pounding fists of the present maintained a relentless banging. She was a pathetic figure, running around the agency trying to prove her vitality, issuing directives, questioning visitors, commenting on procedures she vaguely knew or understood. The quiet contempt built up. Had she known just how scornful the employees were of her vacuous theatrics, she'd have voluntarily retired on the spot. She retained beneath the actress a sensible humanity and a fierce womanly pride. She was a gallant old dame who would have rather walked out a proud old lady than a tearful harridan. The damage she inflicted upon the agency was incalculable. But it wasn't all her own fault. It was directly rooted in Harry's reluctance to remove her from the firing line because of an innocuous, gratuitous sentimentality. Had he really felt genuine affection for her, he would have provided her with the financial means by which she could have retired in well-earned dignity. Or perhaps, he could have arranged to keep her in a limited capacity, somewhere outside the main stream of agency life where she could have won the respect that

88   **Stop!** YOU'RE KILLING THE BUSINESS

someone who had contributed so much to the agency's success
deserved. Harry had witlessly permitted her to become a punching bag and she subconsciously was making the agency pay.

John was 66 and Harry's second oldest employee. He
started as an errand boy and assistant to overburdened Martha.
His driving gut instincts to succeed propelled him and the agency
ahead in great leaps. He was ambitious, and the growth of the
agency meant everything to him; he was our Chapter One Gang
Leader incarnate. Harry refused to retire him too.

John still believed advertising was a "game of contacts."
Few would dispute his view that contacts, as most businessmen
understand the word in proper context, are an immense help in
developing and maintaining customers in any service business.
But they aren't anywhere as critical as good work, delivered on
time, suitable to the needs of the customers.

John saw himself as the U.S. Calvary, circa 1875. When a fat
account became suddenly hostile to agency ideas and the dreary
tidings were reported to Harry, John was dispatched to "smooth
things over, to keep the natives in their places." In the days when
the clients were drinking or whoring buddies of John, this traditional approach often quieted the restless clients. Years later,
however, brand managers or marketing directors with pretty
young wives were often not as interested in screwing or boozing
as their predecessors. They resented John's sudden *deus ex ma-
china* appearances at their meetings in matters about which he
was ill-informed.

Harry stubbornly resisted any attempts to change his policy,
pointing out to anyone who would listen how many accounts
John had saved. John's life would have been considerably more
blissful building nursery furniture for his grandchildren in the
wood shop of his Connecticut farm. But even to the most subtle
suggestions that he consider "easing off," John was affably nega-
tive. "What would Harry do without me?" he said. "This joint
would close in a week." The maker of that myth was, of course,
Harry. It was always Harry, convincing those around him how
great they were because they were part of him.

While Harry professed the indispensability of John and
Martha to anyone in the agency who would listen, in private
conversations with personal friends, he bragged about how he

had "made" them both. Blowing her up to heroic proportions in public, he scorned Martha in private. He called her a "book-keeper." He bragged how he'd made her rich and how she'd be nowhere without him. Pointing to John as his "good strong right hand" in public, he labeled him in private as a "whoremaster peddler." He not only lived with these hypocrisies, he thrived on them.

By keeping them on past their usefulness to the company to satisfy his own egotistical needs, Harry was aging his company instead of making the changes necessary to keep up with the times and the progress of the advertising industry.

Harry's biggest crime, however, was one which cost his agency what it needed most—clients. Harry forbade the passing of any finished work to clients without his personal okay. Most of the time, he never read the copy, so the staff looked at the practice as a harmless little joke. It is true that this innocent ego trip was not a crime in itself, but what was criminal was Harry's continued habit of jamming up work on his desk for days and weeks while clients grew restless. Piles of creative work lay on his desk awaiting his rubber-stamp motion. He often went on trips, leaving layouts for ads with short deadlines unsigned. Instead of confronting him, account men learned to forge his initials and bribed office girls to steal stuff out of his office. A rebellion might have brought on reform, but Harry's men were not at the barricades; they were playing hide-and-seek with their boss and gorging themselves on expense account lunches while they tittered about it among themselves.

Once, an outraged young account man, who would brook no nonsense, finally broke into Harry's locked office one afternoon and was wildly rummaging through the piles of drawings and layouts when Harry's secretary caught him in the act. Before she could unlock her shocked jaw, the young man was slamming his fist down hard on Harry's desk demanding to know where the boss was. After she refused to comply, the man cornered her and in a complete rage, threatened to "rub her out" unless she relented. The scare technique worked. The terrified old biddy gave in and stuttered out the name of a hotel. The young man swung around in Harry's chair and dialed the California number direct.

He reached Harry, who had just come out of a shower and

who was on his way into a poolside meeting with an old crony
from the film business.

"Where the hell is my stuff, you stupid old sonofabitch?"
the young man screamed.

"Calm down, goddamnit," Harry replied. "I took that stuff
to read on the plane. I'll write you my comments, then you can
take it over."

"But I need it now! For tomorrow. The client needs it for
a meeting, you moron!" said the young hothead.

"They waited so long, a few days won't matter," Harry
replied. "Besides, you're fired, you insolent bastard."

Harry, unruffled, returned to his poolside meeting and told
his old buddy that the younger men at the agency couldn't blow
their noses without him.

Harry returned to New York the following week. The disturbed young account man had by now, of course, left the agency
and taken his account with him. Five years later, that account
billed over $1,000,000.

Harry continued to clog up the agency's output by holding
onto the strings of its operation like a master puppeteer. His
recurring response to each loss of a client was a pugnacious
speech to his dwindling band of employees, into which he
sprinkled Churchillian alliteration, urging them on to greater
heights and including a 20-minute narrative of his early life and
times.

As the years slipped by, Ben grew suspicious of Harry's
platitudes and began feeling uneasy about his whole job situation. Regardless of Harry's boundless optimism, the agency
was slipping. Too many younger people were deserting to
join exciting, new, smaller agencies. Too many clients were
beginning to complain that the creative output was dated and
stale. They asked for "creative stuff" like the Alka-Seltzer
commercial or the Benson and Hedges commercial. How
long, in the face of a steady slippage of business, could Harry's legendary reserve hold? Ben began wondering about the
agency's health.

Ben saw a buddy in Accounting who let him look over the

company's financial statements for the past five years. By golly, Harry wasn't such an ass after all. The company did have a good cash reserve; it owned stocks and real estate. Ben already knew that the biggest client in the house was a relative of Harry's who could be counted on in any crisis, but what reassured him now was the very respectable pretax net shown by the agency that year. In an industry where 1% to 2% was considered good, Harry's 7% was miraculous. Somebody was doing something right. Ben's mind was at ease.

Two years later, Harry's five biggest accounts had fled to young, audacious agencies. Harry remained optimistic. He, who was, is, and will always be the eyes, ears, heart, and mind of the agency, would find the way to new business. Everyone knew the jig was up; that is, everyone but Ben.

The day after they lost the Tru-Bloo girdle account, their largest, Harry called Ben into his private office. Weeping with genuine grief, Harry handed Ben a generous ten-week severance check for his ten years' service. Harry explained how he had been done in by conniving, ungrateful employees. He recounted, with portentous drama in his voice, how he must now take to the barricades; once again, alone, he would stand unafraid and re-build his agency. He begged Ben to "stay loose, guy" and "keep in touch, guy" because he just knew it was only a matter of weeks before he was back in action.

Ben staggered out of Harry's office shocked, not so much by the sudden horror of unemployment, but by the realization that all those years Harry's delusions had insidiously seeped into his own head. Harry's trance had entranced him, too.

The agency reserves trickled away and finally it went under and with it any delusions Ben nursed about a long, secure future in the mighty, capable hands of his boss.

Ben has yet to find a real job. The advertising world was not waiting breathlessly for him, despite his good work. He is a bitter man, betrayed by his own instincts which could not see the danger of a boss with a benign egomania. He had failed to see that Harry, whose titanic ego couldn't grasp reality, could murder the business.

A U T O P S Y

Few employees need to consult a home medical advisor to learn how to detect the signs of an ego-crazy boss whose emotional roller coaster rides are ruining the company. Any boss you know, working twelve- and fourteen-hour days, shooting himself like a man out of a cannon to business appointments all over God's little world, single-handedly closing the biggest deals, has got to believe that it is he and he alone who will make or break the annual P and L statement. Nobody has to tell a boss what hard work is about. And nobody should. Employees or bosses can, however, disabuse themselves of all the self-delusion they care to, no matter how assiduously cultivated over the years, if they can remember a few things.

The skills required to start a business are not necessarily the same as those needed to run a business once it is established.

Regardless of how brilliant or versatile he was or is, the boss was more likely than not, substantially helped by one or two behind-the-scenes slaves who shared the crushing work load during the upward climb, during the dark days of struggle, during the sunshine days of success. Only now, the boss's monstrous ego has elected to conveniently forget those little folks in the back office. Nobody but nobody ever builds any business single-handed. Never. Such assertions are clear symptoms of a terminal I.F. mentality.

The purpose of a business is to perform a service or produce a product and earn thereby a profit for its owners in a way satisfying to them. Most businesses start out to reach just that goal. But before too many years have passed, the I.F. mentality obtrudes its heady presence in the office or onto the assembly line and the signals subtly change. The business transforms into the private ego preserve of its owner and founder. The "we's" become "me's." But we know all this, and we are reminded of prestigious tomes, of Ph.D. dissertations written on the subject at America's leading graduate schools of business. What then is the point of further discussion when there seems to be no curative for the corporate ego incarnate?

Here's a handy list to show the Harry of your company. If

you happen to be the Harry yourself and you've recognized yourself on these pages, copy it and carry it around in your wallet between your credit cards.

1] Face it, the business does not need you now as it did when you began it. No matter how you try to rationalize it. No matter how good you are at dissembling. If the business did need you more than ever, you wouldn't need so many capable employees. And if you don't have capable employees around you, the shame is yours, not theirs. Hiring second-raters to fill top jobs is one mental trick you can play on yourself. It makes you feel smarter surrounded by dodos. It enables you to scream and rave all day to yourself about the dolts and idiots who work for you. It reinforces the notion that your are indispensable. It is sheer self-fulfilling prophecy.

2] It may hurt to think of it, but admit it, you didn't build the business with your bare hands. Nobody ever did. Henry Ford had Ernest Breech. Kimberly had Clark. Jones had Laughlin. And they all had hordes of loyal, hardworking, resourceful, sensible, and efficient employees all the way up. That is part of the reason they made it.

3] Finally, if you are honestly past your prime and you've yet to find a rewarding substitute for the challenge of your world in the business world, you have deserved the same epithet hurled by Cromwell to the Rump Parliament on January 22, 1658. He said, "It is not fit that you sit here any longer! . . . You shall now give place to better men."

6

How to Wipe Out the Company Mafia

O U R narrative begins at Ellis Island in the late nineteenth century with the unceremonious arrival of Rudolph Starns from a lower Rhineland town in Germany bearing the usual 16 cents in cash and one million dollars in hope. He also brought a curious old skill learned at his father's tiny shop in Speyer, Germany. He blew elaborately decorated glass hatpins.

His was a boiler-plate American immigrant story. Any other man, at any other era, immigrating to any other country would have been assured of either starving to death as a maker of decorated glass hatpins or of earning his living shoveling manure. But Mr. Starns arrived in a bursting 1867 America where any skill, no matter how remote, found a place. He immediately went into business for himself. The glass hatpin maker soon had a business card stating he was a "Manufacturer of Decorative Accessories for Fine Ladies Millinery Goods." Only in America.

Old Mr. Starns died in 1920, bequeathing his profitable $150,000 per year business to his two sons, Jan and Edgar Starns. The two young men organized themselves. Edgar designed and produced the hatpins, and his brother Jan peddled them on the road for six months a year. The Twenties were tough years for the two young men, but both were adept and the business grew. They branched out into importing floral novelties like birds, bunnies, flowers, and ribbons. By 1925, the brothers concluded that since they were now a fully ripened novelty importing firm (75% of all their sales were imports), it was time they adapted their activities accordingly. They discontinued their manufacturing business; Edgar took over the buying function, traveling three months at a clip throughout Europe while Jan went out each year selling on the road. It was soon apparent that the sweet little girl who answered the telephone and typed invoices could not look after things if both men happened to be away from the office at the same time. So they hired an eager 17-year-old office boy and shipping manager trainee named B. J. Leonard. They romanced young Leonard with promises of a splendidly lit future, provided he was willing to sweat along with them. And they did not lie. As the years streaked past, Leonard rose in measured succession. He was office boy, shipping clerk, assistant office manager, office manager, salesman, regional sales manager, buyer, general manager, and finally, Executive Vice President.

Leonard had been hired at $15 per week in 1925. By 1950, he earned over $50,000 a year and, by 1969, he reached $75,000 a year. His power had increased with his salary, and his pervasive presence was felt from the conference room to the employees' toilets. He did, in fact, inspect the johns periodically. Once he discovered a shipping clerk goofing off in one of the stalls. The young man was pitching cigarette butts into the urinals. Leonard grabbed the kid by the collar from behind, swung him around and thundered, "You keep this goddamn craphouse clean, boy, because I've scrubbed every one of these *pissoirs* with my own hands. I have the cleanest crappers in the building and no slob like you is gonna change that now!" The offender was fired the same afternoon above the protests of the shipping manager who pleaded that the young man was the fastest gun on the shipping line. He appealed over Leonard's head directly to Edgar Starns. Edgar meekly raised the issue with Leonard. Leonard replied, "Either it's that little punk or me!" Edgar caved in immediately and later in the day handed the young man eight weeks' severance pay from a shaking hand.

In addition to everything else, he had also become the arbiter of the petty jealousies and suspicions between the two Starns brothers. The more he fed the fire, the more they leaned on him. So now, at the pinnacle of his power, Leonard had developed ulcers, incipient heart trouble, and an explosively hot temper along with a fat income. It was his contribution to the seven-million-dollar annual volume the firm enjoyed.

His personal life was also sacrificed to the altar of power.

Prolonged absences on company business had produced an indifferent wife and children to whom he was little more than a moneymaking machine. Starns Novelty International had become more than a job; it was a way of life, and he had every scar for the 44 years of work to prove it. He spread-eagled across purchasing, sales, finances, customer control, inventory forecasting, shipping, and product development. His power was so wide-ranging that it had become impossible to manage the business without him. His stranglehold had increased the Starns brothers' dependency on him to the point of rendering their own efforts at management feeble and impotent. When he wasn't present to decide or arbitrate their petty quarrels, everything stopped cold.

After the death of an old uncle, the Starns brothers pledged to end their filial contentiousness. They consulted their accountant who recommended a confidential chat with a management consultant. The man finally forced them to see that their continuing squabbles were impeding the progress of their business. They took good advice and decided to inject professional management, little by little, into their moribund company.

They hired a 34-year-old Marketing Vice President who bore all the tangible operating background necessary to restructure the company's marketing approach for a period of rapid growth. Charles Ames was patient, tolerant, and shrewd—a man with that rare confirmation of mind able to burrow through tangled masses of data and quickly grasp the guts of a tough business problem. Even at $35,000 a year, he was a bargain, having previously run a $2 million-division for a large greeting card manufacturer who had expanded into novelties. Under his tough but sensitive leadership, the division had increased profits ten per cent every year for seven straight years. He managed the division like it was his own business. He was resilient, imaginative, always in control, and sensitive to new approaches. He was a recruiter's dream, and few people around him could understand why he choose to leave his autonomous, secure, well-paid position in the big time to work for the Starns brothers.

Ames knew precisely what he was about. He correctly analyzed the Starns' basic problem after the first interview. It wasn't, as they thought, that years of bickering had taken a heavy toll on the business; the obvious culprit was the vacuum of leadership created and perpetuated by B. J. Leonard. Every polite question Ames asked about who was responsible for what was replied to with a blank stare followed by, "Oh, B. J. takes care of that." Ames quickly sensed a unique opportunity to set the firm back on a straight course and, by it, earn an equity position in the firm, something he could not hope for working for a large corporation. He discussed this with the Starnses, and they shook hands on it.

The irresistible force now moved into position against the immovable object. Ames, the hard-headed, impeccably seasoned young pro wheeled into position for a head-on clash with Leonard, the gallant, battle-worn, old knight. Having foreseen this, Ames had extracted, in advance, a pledge from the Starnses to stand firm behind his decisions no matter what the outcome. It was an underscored precondition of his employ.

Ames, in a mood of calm resolve, set to work, hoping Leonard's vast reserves of experience and insights could be brought in as a positive force in the deployment of a corporate development program. Ames wisely positioned Leonard in his mind as a potentially rich vein of assistance and not as an old warhorse to maneuver out the door.

Ames initial study recommended a phased reorganization of the entire sales management structure as a mandatory prerequisite to a successful five-year plan to double gross annual sales to $14,000,000. Leonard objected vehemently. "His men," as he possessively referred to the sales force, were not school kids. He would not submit his men, he ranted, to the humiliation of filling out patronizingly "dumb sales call report form shit" developed by Ames. He would not stand aside and permit Ames to install a "spy system." Ames calmly rejoined that the system he suggested was primarily designed to speed the flow of sales information back home and thus help reduce chronic out-of-stock conditions which had plagued the company for years and cost it hundreds of thousands in sales every month. Leonard replied that he would not cooperate. Ames pressed his argument. His new system, he said, was not designed to humilate anyone. It merely sought to get an earlier market reaction of certain key items so that the company would have more time to reorder. Leonard remained unmoved. The Starnses sat terrorized as the

two dominant figures slashed at each other. Ames had the last
word. Finally losing his temper, he said, "Your men, B. J., will do
what the company tells them because 'your men' are paid by the
company and not by you." Leonard rose up from his chair fum-
ing. "Go home, you little jerk, screw off, you're finished!" Ames
remained seated. Leonard demanded a decision by the cringing
Starns brothers. They waffled. Ames demanded redemption of
their pledge to him. Either they supported his idea, or they would
have his resignation on the spot. Finally, they timidly gave in and
said they'd give the new system a try. They failed to perceive what
Ames was attempting to accomplish with his plan, but Leonard
was now 63 and Ames was a robust 34. They shamefully made the
right decision for the wrong reasons. Leonard withdrew,
wounded and scandalized.

The conspicuous success of Ames' correctives pushed
Leonard faster into the waiting arms of surly revenge. He began
agitating against Ames with the sales force. He confidentially
aligned certain principal manufacturing sources against Ames
and impugned his integrity by spreading rumors that he was
taking payoffs from their competitors. The Starns' halting decision to support Ames had so devastated him, that he used his best
strategem left; he would now deploy the "family" he had meticulously cultivated over 44 years. He would now cash in all the
markers for juicy territories assigned, for fat raises pushed
through, for summer jobs for college sons and daughters of office
employees. Leonard's machine rallied militantly to his trumpet.
Like a superbly trained commando force, they launched a quick
series of forays against Ames.

Salesmen from all over the country suddenly inundated the
main office with petty complaints about new products developed
by Ames; others merely dogged any items he created. They conveniently forgot to show the samples or distribute catalog sheets
or price lists. The word was out: Sabotage Ames' babies. Overseas factory managers refused to reply to his letters, continuing
to direct correspondence to Leonard. Office personnel gossiped
about Ames' "arrogance" and disdained his stylish young wife
as a snob. In small companies, petty people problems surface
fast. Within his first 4 months on the job, there were more mon-
key wrenches thrown into Ames' department by Leonard's co-

conspirators than into the toolbox of the Ford River Rogue plant
on a Friday night. Ames' machinery predictably sputtered and
slowed down in hopeless confusion.

Leonard's subversion was so brilliantly executed that the
Starnses never suspected they were being had. Ames methodi-
cally explained the events and revealed the culprits. But the
Starnses, nonetheless, remained ineffably niave. How could they
doubt B. J.? How could a man who'd given 44 blood-and sweat-
stained years to the company do such things? They idiotically
demanded that Ames continue to be held accountable for the
frightening pile of screwups. Ames had striven sincerely to ac-
comodate his new programs and policies to Leonard's insecuri-
ties, but he continued to finger Leonard as the gang leader. The
Starnses finally began a quiet investigation of Ames' allegations.
Once again, Leonard assembled his palace guard. Once again,
old loyalties withstood the test in heavy winds. Ames received
uniformly bad grades from salesmen, customers, office personnel, and most of the overseas suppliers. Nobody cared for him.
He was a "Slide Rule Charlie" in a striped tie, a Madison Avenue
Harvard phoney. Ames knew what was happening. He saved the
Starns brothers the embarrassment and submitted his resigna-
tion. It was 5 months from the day he had started work.

Triumphant, Leonard renewed his usual muscle-flexing
methods. The Starnses, now stripped of any hope of professional
personnel from the outside, were more dependant than ever on
him and his gang of cronies who were laced through their company. There was simply no way they could break his power. The
fools had lost control of their own business.

It was soon business as usual at Starns. Ames had prepared
a marketing forecast in which he had predicted a 23% increase
in sales for the fiscal year. The books were closed instead with a
10% decrease. When Edgar Starns looked into this matter with
some alarm, he learned that because the sales department had
failed to communicate early trade reaction on certain new novelty
items that Easter, reorders were placed too late. Nearly all the
salesmen had dogged two key new product lines developed by
Ames. The Starns had become so inured to confusion as a way
of life under Leonard's stewardship, that they naturally accepted
the dismal results as something beyond their control. It didn't

occur to them (although it did years later) that had they deployed Ames' simple recommendations, at least 75% of the reorders could have been shipped and disaster turned into victory.

"That's the breaks of the import business," Leonard said philosophically as the accountants drearily droned out the closing financial report for the year. While Leonard concealed his culpability behind wistful sighs, it was unquestionably he who had planned and executed this masterful destruction. Leonard had, in effect, become a gang leader within the company. Rather than grasping upward for power, Leonard had literally squatted horizontally across nearly every top management function. After 44 years, he held all the strings drawn tightly in his covetous fist. Ames' challenge to that power became a life-and-death threat.

Leonard had sacrificed his family life and his health toiling for the Starnses. The company was his wife, his children, his mistress. He'd replaced the wholesome security pegs of family with a feudal system of blood-sworn loyalties founded on a constant exchange of favor and spoils. The company was his private fief, manipulated to satisfy his sick ego and not the aspirations of the ownership. Ames was a threat to the very substance of Leonard's life and had to be eliminated quickly and efficiently. In typical, 1933 Chicago gang warfare style, Leonard had put out a contract on Ames.

It now remained to be seen if conditions would return to the norms Leonard perceived as secure, or whether Ames' brief tenure had jarred the Starnses from their lethargy. As events were to turn out, a calm return to bumbling as usual would have been a blessing compared with what then unfolded.

A nagging suspicion continued to haunt Edgar Starns' nights. Could Ames' allegations have not had even a tiny seed of truth? He'd never really know, he thought, unless he repeated the whole elaborate process of covert recruiting, hiring an new man, and observing with greater care. He telephoned his brother one night. A vitriolic exchanged ensued during which each blamed the other for Ames' sudden departure.

They finally agreed to try again. This time, they eschewed outsiders. They dipped into the family instead, pulling out a benign rotten apple: Edgar Starns' younger son, Roger, who'd been nursing a meager law practice but thriving like a prince on a generous annual dividend from the family firm. Roger agreed to come into the business. He felt that at 33 it was time to lay aside the heavy burdens of ski weekends at Aspen and summers in Sardinia with French movie starlets and prove to the whole family that he had more than Jack Daniels in his blood. One week later, the Starnses solemnly announced the official entrée of Roger as Chief Operating Officer in Training. Edgar, now more wary, admonished Leonard to extend to Roger every inch of the dedication he had delivered to them. Leonard left his office giggling. He returned after lunch announcing he heartily endorsed the choice of heir apparent. He knew Roger was a harmless lightweight and no threat to anything that moved.

When Roger showed up for work the first day, he immediately inducted him into the gang by assuring him he had nothing to worry about. "I'm behind you 100 per cent" Leonard said. Anything screwed up, he was to come to his "Uncle" Leonard. This was great news to Roger. He was a man who was known to have traveled 10,000 miles, changing planes three times, just to sleep with a particularly succulent young lady, but it soon became apparent that he would not travel 10 miles out of his way to see a new customer. He rapidly fell comfortably under Leonard's avuncular dominance.

Roger assumed greater and greater tokens of power as time rolled on, making largely ceremonial appearances in the Far East, at trade conventions, and at sales meetings. He enjoyed the illusion of power Leonard had created for him. Leonard had meanwhile continued with his 44-year-old juggling act, stumbling deeper and deeper into a bottomless pit of management responsibilities. Sales declined steadily as the months rolled on.

The Starns brothers, who had begun reducing their daily work load when Roger had passed his 90-day trial period, sensed they had fumbled again. They helplessly watched their net worth dwindle because they were simply too tired and disgusted either to replace Roger or stop Leonard. Their parochial upbringing had severely limited their capacity to think conceptually and many obvious alternatives were foreclosed by their now stubborn insistence of "keeping things in the family" no matter what the cost.

But their life's work hung in the balance. Their accountants admonished them to act in some way to bind the bleeding wounds. They didn't know which way to turn, and they were such totally vacuous men that they decided to sell the business. Leonard refused to hear anything of it. There was nothing wrong with the business, he said, that could not be cured by one "hot new item." He upbraided the two brothers for losing faith in themselves and in him. But this time, with their eyes glued on the alarming trickle of net worth, they turned stone deaf to his pleas. For the first time in their lives, when their capital was threatened, they began at last to act like bosses. Discreet feelers were put out in the industry. Like a sheet of paper floating down to earth in a spring breeze, word of the Starns' desire to make a fast deal settled quietly on the desk of none other than Mr. Charles Ames.

After the Starns debacle, Ames' old company had rehired him warmly. The practical insights he'd gained during his brief tenure at Starns had not dimmed his enthusiasm for the novelty importing business. With an eye to acquisition, he efficiently activated his intelligence network. He learned that the Starns brothers were anxious to get out fast and that Roger Starns, an ineffective figurehead, was drinking at the helm. Ames prepared a plan and set it before the board of his company. They would tender a generous offer to buy out the Starnses and, if successful, graft it onto Ames' own novelty division. This plan would then have given Ames Division a desirable beachhead in the import field at a price one-tenth of what they figured as the entry fee of starting from scratch.

The company management accepted the idea and authorized Ames to proceed on his own to acquire Starns. Ames hired a cat's-paw management consultant to make the initial approach to Roger Starns. The offer of a quick sellout at what seemed a generous price above net worth sent Roger scrambling around the world after his vacationing father and uncle. They eagerly returned within a few days.

Negotiations passed from the tentative stage to the serious deliberation of terms and when the final negotiations ensued, Charles Ames stepped out from the shadow and revealed himself and his company as the mysterious "principal." Embarrassed, but too anxious to concern themselves about form, the Starnses admitted to being flattered by Ames' attentions and blandishments of hot, immediate cash on the barrelhead. Ames refrained from rekindling any old flames about Leonard. But he did state, from the start, his unequivocal intention to heave B. J. Leonard out the front door as soon as the ink was dry on the contract. Primal revenge was involved to some extent. Ames would not have been human had he not relished the delicious revenge that lay before him. But his decision was sound, based on his correct assessment that Leonard was an anachronism, a gang leader, and the major management problem of the business. By now panting for the money, the Starnses' reply to Ames' resolve to kick out Leonard was a feeble nod. They agreed not to reveal news of the sale until the day of closing lest Leonard launch another devastating commando attack out of sheer rage.

It was now time for the Starns brothers to relieve their dual conscience. They met in private one night and decided to bestow a fat severance check on Leonard as payment for his years of service. They agreed on 1 year's salary, $75,000. Calculated against the average of overtime and weekends Leonard spent fumbling around with company business each year, the sum worked out to about $10 an hour over 44 years, which was about what the men in the warehouse earned for overtime during the busy seasons of the year. In order to gain the tax advantage, however, they gave Leonard the money in one lump sum. Taxwise this meant that Leonard would be lucky to net half, about $35,000. Of course, no provisions could be made to repay Leonard for his ulcer-riddled stomach, his shattered nerves, his bleak family life, and his youth.

It certainly could have been worse. Lots of guys get gold watches for more and lots get bottles of cologne for not much less. But there was no check in the world fat enough to cover 44 years of a life lost, of a neurotic wife, of scornful and indifferent daughters. So when Edgar Starns handed Leonard the check after a luncheon at a fine restaurant where he was told the news, Leonard grew glassy-eyed and broke down.

They fed him and wined him and poured martinis down him and invited him to retire and visit with them at their summer homes, but he sat staring into his coffee cup. They patted him on the back and discreetly left him to himself. B. J. Leonard walked around the city that night thinking about that gratuitous piece of paper in his wallet. Starns Novelty International had been his life. It was now gone. And it was apparent to him that there was no reason for him to continue either. He threw himself beneath the wheels of a subway train that night, happy at the end that he had cheated Charles Ames of the pleasure of showing him the door.

Charles Ames attended the funeral with the Starnses and the following day hit the company like a one-man Panzer Division. He fired 15 people the first day, 20 the second, and nearly a total of 40 by week's end. This predictably threw matters into chaos. Ames had expected this when he had predicted the losses for the first quarter, but his plan now began operating. Ames had replaced old men and old systems where necessary and retained old men and old systems where they worked well. Merchandise flow dramatically improved through a penalty system with sources of supply on late orders. Salesmen worked against a generous new incentive plan of company stock. A new team of designers brought in a new line thoroughly tested to tickle public fancy. At the close of the fiscal year, the division earned a record profit. Three years later, sales had been doubled and net operating profits increased by an incredible 100%.

Ames admits now that the plan which transformed Starns from a sinking, sluggish old scow into a vital, moneymaking ocean liner was, in fact, the verbatim master plan he had originally submitted to the Starns brothers while he was their employee. Ames' company paid $850,000 in cash and stock for the Starns importing business, and another $450,000 for the building in which the company operated. He feels today that had the Starns brothers stood behind him and given him the scope he was promised and held Leonard and his gang in check, the business would have been worth over $7,000,000 within 3 years. The Starns brothers' timidity, coupled with Leonard's stranglehold on the inner mechanics of company operations, had killed their business and cost the brothers nearly 6 million dollars.

AUTOPSY

"Gang warfare" can bump off any business, or, at the least, bloody it. The case revealed here is commonplace. There are infinite variations on the theme. Perhaps a fading sales manager whose contacts with the trade are so jealously guarded becomes irreplaceable because there is a risk of serious loss of business attached to his departure. Every so often, our typical gang chieftain grows up from a quiet, little night-school girl of 19, who begins as assistant bookkeeper when a business is young, and who ripens into a screaming but indispensable middle-aged harridan when the business grows up. Now in supreme power, she cows employees with her voice or her shaking index finger. She can't be fired because she alone holds 1,000 tiny keys to doors that open the main entrance to the daily functioning of the company.

She's a "Leonard" too, because after 25 or 30 years or so, there's hardly a soul around who doesn't owe her something—most of all the bosses. After all, she continually reminds them, didn't she give them her youth?

But who is really guilty? Who really deserves to be booked for this type of company murder? Power-hungry loyal old employees who meticulously build empires? Hardly. We can indict ownership. It stands accused and convicted of these felonies beyond any reasonable doubt.

We accuse lazy ownership.

We accuse permissive ownership which allows horizontal squatting on too many management functions by a single, well-meaning, power-crazy zealot.

We accuse ownership which places a higher value on loyalty and sweat than on brains and integrity and loses the basic message of business. Any boss who encourages his executive or managerial staff to play cheap heroics because he equates long, lonely hours of unpaid overtime with saintly moral acts is going to pay a heavy price for these pretensions someday. Hell hath no fury like a saint scorned.

Is this an insidiously disguised case for power to the bosses? Not really. Loyalty, blood, toil, sweat, tears, and so forth are often truly significant measurements of an employee's true value to his boss. They are not, however, even trade-offs for common sense, cooperativeness, and willingness to perfect a single job at a time. Management should recognize and reward that kind of employee promptly. Too many bosses prefer to count the number of crumpled coffee containers on a man's desk the next morning.

If you happen to work for a company which values attributes like laughing on cue at the boss's jokes or working late just to look good, you would be well advised to resign soon. You may just create an empire like B. J. Leonard. You'd be far better off being the best sales manager, or shrewdest purchasing agent, or the most speedily perfect carpet installer in a firm that values special skills over coruscating virtuosity.

Owners should be sure that their employees are doing the jobs for which they are best suited. A salesman whose boss thinks he has a talent for purchasing can't sell when he's learning about purchasing, and a purchasing man can't buy when he's preoccupied with the implanted notion that he has a "natural sales personality."

It happens every day. Merchandising people who are supposed to create and produce the goods must take to the road to sell them becuase they've failed to impart enough of themselves to the salesmen so the salesmen can't sell. And what do the salesmen do? Naturally, they sit around in offices writing the merchandising people memos about merchandising. Precious hours, long, dreary meetings, eating up golden moments ticktocking away into eternity any chance for the company to survive the first competitive battle. Production men scurrying around the country selling and salesmen sitting around writing about what's wrong with the products.

Keeping good people productively in place isn't easy. But it's the single, most effective deterrent to gang warfare in the company. If you don't want a B. J. Leonard "& Co." to gang up on you or your company, make these simple rules into simple policy:

1] If a man is an effective salesman with superior management potential, don't waste time teaching him general management. Wait till he becomes a great salesman first. Then decide if his management potential is so enticing that you are willing to trade off his proven ability for the larger objective of assuring the flow of new talent into management.

2] If you have a B. J. Leonard working for you and you can't find a way to cut him down to size without feeling like Judas Iscariot, try this first. Insist he take an expensive, long overdue month's vacation. While he's away, every menacing weakness in your organization will show up like chicken pox in the morning within a week. Every wrestling hold he has on his twenty "jobs" will be quickly revealed. Within two weeks, everyone in the office will be helplessly running around screaming, "Oh god, Leonard's the only one who knows about that." Workmen with 30 years on the job will forget where the tools are kept. Purchase orders on urgently needed materials will lie unsigned on desks. No other person would dare sign anything. Accounts payable won't know whom to pay first. Shipping won't know which salesman gets which samples. Customers inquiring about their orders or their appointments will received embarrassed shrugs in return. Sooner or later, long before your B. J. Leonard returns, some irate customer will scream through the phone in an ear-breaking din, "Who the hell is in charge there?"

Then, when your helpless employees cry out for help, ask them why. Why do they need help?

Give them the responsibility. On the spot, without reservations, tell them to do it, right or wrong, and not to worry about B. J. Leonard. Tell them they are forbidden from disturbing Leonard during his vacation. You'll find that the people you've underestimated can get the job done. It's Leonard's power and your acceptance of it which has made both them and you blind to their capabilities. You can now assign the jobs permanently to the people best suited to handle them. Don't delay.

When your B. J. Leonard returns, expect him to be insufferable and stridently curious about why things were done in a particular way during his vacation. "Why was this done this way, we never do it this way," he'll shout at the clerks. "Why were the number 23 gizmos orders without washers? Why was the display room changed around? Why did the samples go out without my approval? Who gave you permission to install a desk-top copying machine?" Instruct all employees involved to reply to such questions with one answer, "Boss's orders. He didn't want you disturbed."

If B. J. Leonard comes crashing into your office complaining bitterly, tell him it was high time he eased his burden anyway. Tell him you expect him to take at least two long vacations a year hereafter. Tell him he never looked so hale and hearty. He'll either get the drift at once or force you, with his protests, to take the next step.

Hire a strong, seasoned assistant for Leonard. Someone with solid experience in your business. Someone who shapes up like a real threat to his paranoid fear of competitors for the venerated spot of Company Hero Number One. Leonard will undoubtedly explode. Hold your ground. Don't fire the assistant. Merely assign him a few of the smaller jobs Leonard was doing previously. Place him under your direct supervision. Leonard will then be forced into making a brutal choice. Either he accepts an assistant reporting to him or allows the potentially dangerous new person to report directly to you. Either way, Leonard's wings are clipped with controllable fireworks. If you can't manage ploy two, you must then bite the bullet. You tell your Leonard directly that either he breaks up his gang or you're going to bust him right out the door, 20 years of loyal service or not. You may be surprised to find how few men, given the choice, would resign.

3]   If underestimating the talents of employees is a mistake, remember that overestimating them is just as fatal a misjudgment. There is a natural tendency in any business for power to flow upward to the people who are willing to hack out the most work. This doesn't mean that they are the most talented.

     There's another tendency among ownership to approve of the way an employee is "taking hold" in so many diverse functions. In its often cheap little mind, ownership thinks it's getting a fantastic bargain when they've got one employee seemingly doing the work of three. In such cases, management is cheating itself. If the company publicly proclaims a talented advertising manager is a purchasing genius because the man buys offset printing so efficiently, the ad manager will quickly be sending memos to the purchasing department suggesting ingenious ploys or inventive new methods for getting better prices on electric bulbs or Kotex for the machines in the ladies toilets. Before you can control things, your indignant purchasing man will be spending half the day nosing around the advertising department, flooding it with trenchant memos on means of promoting your lousiest products.

If your ad manager, or purchasing man, or mail boy is really good, tell him. Give him a raise. If he clearly understands that his progress at the company hangs on his perfection of his own, not anyone else's job, he'll establish a department for you and not an empire.

4] If you have an unusually bright, doggedly loyal, diligent jewel of an employee who'd be murder to replace, force yourself to reflect on his motivations. Is he trying to perfect his job or amass power? If you can sniff out a power play, try shorting it by making him a gift of minority equity in the company. Ownership tends to curb a man's appetite for raw power. At the heart of all power plays is the possessiveness hidden in a man's soul—that is the hard core of what "Leonarding" is about. Such men literally want to possess the business. As a minority stockholder, an employee's whole viewpoint radically shifts. No matter how small the equity, his thirst has been quenched. He doesn't need the power anymore; his behavior in the office will reflect his new sense of security and inner freedom. Petty office infighting will no longer suit his status as a minor aristocrat; he will lose interest in it.

Sharing a bit of equity is far cheaper in the long run than what this very special employee's madness as a mature Leonard will cost you. Perhaps, if B. J. Leonard had been given stock equity, no matter how small, things would have been different. At least one thing seems certain: If his final payoff of $75,000 had been in the form of company stock rather than a final, gratuitous guilt gesture, he might not have ended his life beneath the wheels of a subway train.

In big companies, they call power plays "top level management problems." How do they solve them? They pump more money down the drain because they can't change course as quickly as you can. When they finally slow down to a halt, a few guys are fired; a few million are lost. And plants, machines, or investments are written off and out of the annual report.

But you don't have $6 zillion and three years to take heavy tax write-offs. So you'd better be careful about how often, why, and which backs you pat. The back you pat today may be that of the man who'll be heading the company Mafia next year.

7

How to Bleed to Death, Drop by Drop

I K N O W a man who loved to diversify his small business. Every product was a sleeper. Every idea buried in his cluttered desk drawer was a potential moneymaker. This guy's nuttiness had a real kinky dimension; he loved to form companies to diversify. Just like some guys will fight, others will drink, and still others jump into bed with any stray alley cat, this guy loved to call his lawyer and form a company right on the spot. He loved the snap of stock certificates in his hand; he loved the idea of being Chairman of the Board, Treasurer, Secretary, and loved making his wife Vice President. By the time he was 40, he'd formed 30 different corporations to develop product variations in his dry cleaning supplies business. Stacked together, all of them didn't have as many assets as a kid's lemonade stand on a muggy summer Sunday.

While obviously an idiotic waste of his lawyer's time and fees, this screwball's fetish didn't harm his business. He'd form the corporation, get the by-law books gold-stamped, and stack them in a glass book shelf behind his desk. When you came to talk to him, he'd always point at the glass bookcase stuffed with corporations and say with grinning pride, "How do you like my little conglomerate?"

Unfortunately, this same psychological wrinkle runs through the minds of rational men too. The compulsion to solve tough business problems by diversifications bought at the low cost of either forming a "division" or a subsidiary or mostly just plunking down a few innocent bucks to research a new field is irresistible to a surprising number of otherwise careful businessmen.

Because a diversification move is often cheap and because, at the outset, it hardly seems to involve anything more than shifting a few numbers and a few bodies, too many people do it. And they should stop doing it, because it is dumb.

And who are the prime offenders? The smartest people you know, of course. A person like Robert Enders for example, who had a company called Climax Electronics.

During those early, booming years of the mid-Fifties, when the military-industrial complex was reaching adolescence, a mild, scholarly, bachelor engineer named Robert Enders was running a quietly prosperous electronics job shop in a sleepy town at the suburban edge of Eastern Long Island, New York.

Enders' operations centered around the larger electronics manufacturers in the area from whom he drew small subcontracts. These firms were, in turn, subcontractees of defense giants. Enders was far removed from the fast-moving world of defense contract procurement, bidding, and multimillion dollar transactions. He employed 15 superbly skilled technicians, many of whom were postwar refugees from war-ravaged Europe. His company's work bore the unmistakable stamp of his scrupulous attention to detail and perfection of product to the minutest detail. His deliveries were without exception perfect, prompt, and cheery. His personal manner was warm, cooperative, practical; he never pushed for work but preferred to stand on his untarnished record of achievement for the companies with whom he worked. Purchasing agents respected his high degree of professionalism and gave him an increasing share of their business in his particular field. Enders was 39 in 1957. Defense contracting was exploding on Long Island. The world was a very nice place indeed.

By the close of 1957, Enders assumed his first large-scale job, a direct contract from Global Aeronautics, one of the biggies of the American defense industry, and to help execute it, hired Kenneth McBain, Ph.D., his first full-time research engineer.

With a continuing unblemished record of excellence and a back-up engineer of broad scope, Enders was now encouraged by purchasing agents to continue seeking bigger jobs and to begin thinking about assuming more sophisticated activities in the field of Research and Development.

By 1961, Enders and McBain had moved into the $1,000,000-volume class and Climax Electrical Shop & Services was rechristened Climax Electronics, Inc. Enders was now 43, living comfortably in a 100-year-old stone cottage in a picturesque village twenty miles from his plant. He spent most of his leisure time fishing off a modest sailboat and pursuing healthy male activities with his fiancee of 15 years, whom we shall call Helen the Secretary. Yet, all was not sublime in the mind of Robert Enders. He was bothered by an instinctive stirring in his mind, a nudging, an annoying feeling that somehow, the party would not last forever. Robert Enders was a man who abhorred surprises. He didn't want to be the last to know that defense spending would be pared by Kennedy. He was worrying nights and began discussing his apprehension with Ken McBain.

He was, by nature, a careful meticulous man. He believed those stories he'd read in trade publications about growing defense budgets, blossoming plants, new vistas opening, but all the hyperbole of the trade press could not convince him cold. He was worried about the rebellious taxpayers. He was worried about the young new President's policies, and he worried about the capriciousness of the industry in what he rightly guessed was its fickle youth.

McBain disagreed in principle with Enders, but he had come to respect Enders' instincts. He agreed that a thorough investigation of nondefense-related electronic projects could do no harm and, for the cost involved, was probably a good investment.

After long weeks of pouring over countless ideas, Enders and McBain narrowed their options down to three possible "go" fields: consumer TV antennas as an end-use product in stores, flight monitoring equipment for small airports, and aficionado, quality, amateur ham radio equipment. Each field was discussed at length, the men weighing the merits of equally appealing possibilities. The final choice, however, was made for a reason which never once entered the discussion, no less the minds of the two men during their tortured deliberations.

Helen the Secretary, suddenly and inexplicably, got tired of waiting. She would no longer tolerate her relationship with Enders on the old basis. She confronted him in the early spring of 1962 at a knockdown showdown right in his Spartan office decorated only with a large portrait of his Labrador Retriever, Rippin.

Helen struck out with accusations wildly, suggesting he had used her, used her body, drained her youth, wasted her time. She was tired, she said, of playing what had become a lifetime role of mistress to a man who wasn't even married. She'd decided, the week before, having hit her 35th birthday, that the party was over.

Thunderstruck by this sudden rebellion, Enders characteristically asked for several weeks to think things through. Helen shot back. "For God sakes, Robbie, for once in your goddamned life, will you make a decision emotionally! Please, I am not a piece of circuitry, I am your piece of ass," she thundered, stomping out of the room.

Plagued with guilt, wracked by sexual torment, befuddled by this uncharacteristic outburst he could never have forecast, Enders capitulated. He forced himself to admit, finally, that he truly loved Helen the Secretary. And that while he preferred the present arrangement because it better suited his sense of order, he would ask for her hand, goddammit.

In July 1962, Enders was on his way to Jamaica on a honeymoon cruise, doing with Helen what he had been doing with Helen for 15 years—but this time sanctioned by the piece of paper in Helen's hand. His rapid capitulation had pleased and shocked his bachelor cronies. He'd had a reputation as the most successfully evasive bachelor in their set.

Enders and his bride interwove their amours with idle speculation about the future of Climax Electronics. Beneath the gently swaying palms, Helen then veered off the topic of business and dropped a bomb: She wanted to become a mother.

Enders froze in shock. He'd understood her to have agreed that since they were both edging into middle age, a family would be out of the question. Helen insisted that they try.

Whether this sudden shift in signals would indeed produce an heir was not as immediately pressing on Enders' mind as the mere thought of an heir. In the semiperfect world that was his mind, in those quietly oiled filing cabinets in his head, he placed a new set of alternatives. If he was to be a daddy at 44, he had to be doubly sure that his heir was amply provided for. This meant, of course, in his male chauvinist mind, that if a boy came, he'd need room for him in the business. And that meant achieving a bigger, broader volume base than he'd previously discussed with McBain. Having been content with a small kingdom, he now sought an empire.

As his ship sailed full speed ahead back to New York, the final decision as to how Climax would go was already forming in his mind. Now, added to that, events at home conspired to cooperate. McBain had suddenly broken through on a pet research project: a superior low-cost home TV antenna. They had, finally, a consumer product worthy of the skills of Climax.

Within a year, the Radar-Rota Superantenna had moved from McBain's head into the testing lab and from there was distributed in appliance stores all over the Northeast. It was a product of which Enders could be proud. The painstaking process of manufacturing a quality product paid handsomely. By 1964, the antenna was producing sales of $400,000 a year and throwing off a handsome net profit.

The quick success of the Radar-Rota was publicized throughout the trade by that singular grapevine of exaggeration called salesmen. Appliance salesmen threw figures around like discounts. The watchful eyes of the electronics importers now began squinting for a closer look. It was not an easy item to knock off. Nor was it that complex. The crucial factor here was that the importers could make their inexpensive Far East copies look like the Radar-Rota so that people would think it was a Radar-Rota even though it would never perform like a Radar-Rota. First one small importer copied the antenna, bringing into the country 1,000 antennae in early 1965. They were a rapid sellout. And as is so often the case in Far Eastern success, the word spread like wildfire to every tiny antenna company in Hong Kong, Taiwan, and Japan. By 1966, 15 copies of the antenna were being imported, flooding into mass discount stores at $9.99 while Radar-Rota languished in neighborhood appliance stores at $24.95.

This process began choking off Climax volume by March 1967, when projected sales of $35,000 for the month came in at $25,000. His sales people lamented Enders' refusal to introduce a cheaper model of their own made in the Far East under the Radar-Rota name. The carping and criticism failed to budge Enders. He stood strongly on his ground. He absorbed the competitive shock waves well and, by year's end, reported sales of

$700,000 on the item. This satisfied him, but not his sales people, who had looked for a $1,000,000-year.

While the grumbling continued unabated, Enders repaired to his workshop at home to once again consider what he'd learned over the past 3 years. He called McBain again. And together, the two men disappeared into the country home of Enders to consider their situation. Should they send the product for duplication to the Far East? Would they be chopped up by importers no matter how they debased the product? They concluded they would be. They decided to continued marketing Radar-Rota as a unique product within levels of anticipated profits and affordability. But they were now convinced that the need to diversify was upon them once more.

They decided to expand the company's proven capacity to produce high-caliber antennas by entering the profitable radio hobbyist market. So Climax proceeded with the carefully plotted development of a line of FM antennae, ham radio antennae, and short-wave specialties. These products enjoyed mild, but not significant, success. Crucial to Enders, however, was the fact that his nondefense-related sales volume was now $900,000.

Thereafter, in his characteristically tendentious way, Enders moved into broadening segments of the hobbyist field and eased into making emergency two-way radio systems for law enforcement use. His 1968 sales were: defense-related, $1,500,000; nondefense, $1,000,000.

Enders' original instincts had been sound. His painstaking diversification, begun 6 years before, was paying off. He became one of those envied men with a solid business, in control of growth, and without the need for huge infusions of outside capital. His competitors, who were now drowning in a turbulent sea of diminishing defense contracts, struggled with financial problems, stock issues, skyrocketing diversification costs, and increasing skepticism about the future. At the close of 1969, Climax' sales remained stagnant, but here was the volume mix now: defense-related, $1,000,000; nondefense, $1,500,000.

He'd built his house of brick and no wolf in the form of a parsimonious Congress was going to blow his house down in a tempest of defense spending cuts. He was safe. But for Robert Enders, safe was not safe enough. He had to be sure. That meant to him, a 100% conversion to nondefense and moreover, a doubling of sales volume during the following three years. It was while he wrestled with these two major tasks that he met the legendary Harlow J. Stevens, and Robert "the careful" Enders embarked on a slow, scenic journey on the unpaved road to the commercial grave.

Stevens was a retired electronics magnate from the West Coast whom Enders had met at a trade convention. He was now doubling that wealth by building immense retirement communities all over the Sun Belt of the United States. He was tinkering and dabbling, but his touch was so golden that everything he began turned profitable. His reputation for astounding foresight was well deserved. Enders treated him with near reverence and was shocked and surprised when the old man returned the compliment by saying he'd heard lots of good things about Climax from friends in the industry back East.

When he suggested Enders have dinner with him that evening, the flattered engineer could not have been in a more heavenly state. But if he was flying before dinner, Enders reached an exquisite high as he and Stevens clinked ponies of brandy while the waiter cleared the dishes in the dimly lit steak house. Stevens so strongly believed in quality and resourcefulness that he was ready to offer Enders an unparallelled opportunity. Enders nervously tamped out his freshly begun cigar as he began listening.

Stevens was and had always been entranced by the idea of pay TV. The pay TV boom of the late Fifties and mid-Sixties had waned because of the tremendous upsurge of educational television and the rather lackluster performance of test pay TV systems already extant. Moreover, Community Antenna Television Systems were mushrooming all over the nation. This unique industry, which sells subscriptions to master antenna hookups like electric or gas utilities in areas where natural obstructions like mountains limit reception quality, had, to a great extent, broadened the prospects of pay TV outside the regular broadcast channels. But Stevens believed in pay TV for reasons other than bringing Don Giovanni to the 12,000 citizens of his Vista Real community in the southwest. He saw it as a possible substitute for the retail store and the Sears catalog rolled into one.

Stevens believed that the costs of operating retail outlets

had grown so prohibitive and the mindless, massive crush of humanity in chain stores had so diluted the once pleasant diversion of shopping, that millions of people were ready to shop by TV. TV had already proven a dynamic medium for selling. There were enough advertising success stories to fill ten libraries. The media, the selling techniques, and the people who mastered them already existed in the nation's advertising agencies. The networks were in the business of selling time. All that was needed was a reply mechanism which could be installed in a television set and connected to a central data facility which could record the order, process it, and move it to a central warehouse for processing and shipping.

Stevens secret plan was called Buy TV. Its ostensible purpose was to provide a dazzling array of high-priced entertainment events free to subscribers, provided these people permitted the Buy TV company to install boxes in their homes. Stevens was convinced that if people got first-run movies, opera, and sporting events for nothing, they'd definitely buy goods right off the screen from national mail order sellers who would buy time to sell their wares. The Buy TV profit was to come from a 30% share of the sales of all merchandise as payment for the TV time.

This is not the place for technical or theoretical discussion of the Stevens Buy TV plan. Whether it was the whimsical dream of a bored old man who happened to be rich, or an idea with practical possibilities is unimportant. What is instructive is that it seemed real enough to the practical, logical mind of Robert Enders.

Stevens told Enders that the problem with Buy TV lay only in the perfection of the answer-back device which would be installed in the home. The Buy TV system was a scramble system broadcast on standard TV channels, utilizing one national channel on which nonsubscribers would simply receive horizontal jitters, phase inversions, or audio interference. The system required nothing more than a standard home antenna and a small unit inside a TV set, something which Climax could develop.

Enders could hardly believe that this great personage was offering his tiny speck of a company a contract to develop a crucial part of a great pay TV system. Stevens wasn't. He was offering Enders the assignment, at his own expense, of developing the answer-back unit for Stevens, with a signed contract stating that when the first working prototype and set of production drawings were delivered, Stevens would organize a corporation for $20 million and Enders would receive 15% of the outstanding nonissued public shares for his efforts. Stevens further promised to provide complete details of all the work done to date by his own company and also pay the travel expenses of any one of his own engineers whom Enders might need to advance the project.

Enders returned home excited. Stevens' plan offered exactly what he was looking for—a chance to make big money at what seemed a very low level of risk. He wrote Stevens requesting more information to evaluate before making a final decision. Stevens immediately complied. Cases of documents, schematic drawings, charts, and brochures arrived within days accompanied by a man named Berjan who was Stevens' chief engineer. Berjan met with the Climax group in a top-secret conference at Enders home. He seemed a sound, lucid, knowledgeable man. He had left a very well paying job at a large California aerospace company to join Stevens' venture group.

Berjan left New York two days later, having answered most of the questions to the general satisfaction of the Climax management. Enders and McBain (now Enders' partner) undertook a cost analysis of the project themselves. It was their money and essentially their decision whether to go or not, so they took full responsibility and called in no staff. They wanted secrecy, and they didn't want any lower-level executive errors in judgment to hurt their chances.

To their amazement, they learned that the project, far from being a half-baked fantasy, had advanced to a relatively final phase. Moreover, the device assigned to them, it seemed, would not require more than $30,000 to produce during the first year of development. The money seemed a small price to pay for such a monumental moneymaking project. They rechecked and double-checked their figures and estimates. There was no way they could see that the Buy TV project could cost them more than $30,000 the first year, and since Enders' insistence on tough money management had assured a respectable accumulation of cash in the business, the $30,000 seemed like no money at all. They were further disarmed, when during a telephone conversation with Stevens from his yacht off Catalina Bay, the old man offered to defray half of Climax's costs during the first year as a gesture of good will. No stranger to a gift horse, Enders quickly accepted Stevens' generous offer and agreed on a deal over the phone.

The following week, Climax went to work on Buy TV, before first drafts of the contracts were even exchanged by Stevens' and Enders' lawyers. Climax was first to evaluate five answer-back systems already developed, select the most practical, and manufacture 1,000 units as part of a test being planned for the following year's end.

In early 1970, the project was advancing on schedule. By the end of the year, Enders' projection had proved precise. The project had cost his company $30,000 plus or minus five percent. He dutifully mailed Stevens an invoice for $15,000 and was promptly paid.

He now evaluated what he had. They had narrowed the systems down to two. It would take another year to work out which of the alternatives was most desirable. Once again Enders budgeted the project. The Little Black Box project, as it came to be called because of the color and the highly secret nature of the prototypes used, required another man to speed the final analysis of the two types. So Enders budgeted $50,000 for R & D in 1971, hardly a figure calculated to make anyone blink in an electronics company which was now in the $3,000,000 sales bracket.

During 1971, Enders' old foreboding finally came to pass. The reduction of aerospace budgets and the scandals on cost overruns had taken a deadly toll on the defense contracting industry. Enders had indeed become a prophet in his own time. He saw his own company's military sales slide to $400,000. Out of his consumer products and hobbyist divisions had come the largest single producer of sales and profits. Satisfied that he had sustained his small company by astute management, he spent the Little Black Box budget for 1971 without a second thought. Fifty thousand would not take him down the tank.

At the end of 1971, all concerned agreed on the final working answer-back system, and Climax began to develop the prototype of a complete, self-contained unit for installation into potential millions of TV sets.

Now, however, the Little Black Box project began getting hungrier. Estimates for 1972 costs now ranged between $100,000 minimum to $150,000 maximum. At this point, Enders plunged into the decision-making mode so many company presidents and owners have entered for decades.

Thus far, Climax had brought the project forward to a point where completion was in sight. But how far along was Stevens on his end? A flurry of reports back and forth indicated that Stevens' group had progressed about as fast as Climax and they were on target for a proposed 1972 site test.

What did the situation for 1972 look like? Estimates indicated costs would rise to $200,000 by then. Nothing to get alarmed about, but certainly, by the end of 1973, Climax would have spent a total of $500,000 on the Little Black Box without the first penny back. What was Stevens doing on financing? Stevens flew his own chief financial officer East. This man was also a retired millionaire with impeccable credentials in the banking field. He indicated to Enders that four banks had pledged up to $5,000,000 upon completion of the Buy TV test at Villa Real and that Stevens had personally contracted to match it with all his subcontractees with $5 million of his own, to finance a national corporation to begin Buy TV.

How could Enders complain? What was his piddling few dollars among this mass of capital? All input completed, Enders signed off $100,000 for 1972 but told his chief Little Black Box engineer that a penny past the budgeted amount was to be reported at once. Midway through the year, the Little Black Box ran into its first snag. One of Stevens' engineers had developed an idea for a response system far superior to what Climax was now busy producing. Stevens was so enthused by the new idea that he personally flew East with the man to demonstrate it to Enders. Everyone agreed the new idea took far greater advantage of the state of the art and technology in computer hookups than the final system previously approved. It might cost just a bit more, but the results would be well worth it.

Enders agreed, but he also asked what he was going to do with the accumulated time, effort, hardware, and people now. Stevens offered to go half on the additional cost. Enders, his gut instincts slowly awakening, reluctantly agreed.

The "minor redesign" involved in the new system cost $250,000; Climax's share: $125,000, or $25,000 over budget. Backtracking on all the previously completed work cost another $50,000. Enders faced fiscal 1972 with growing apprehension.

His nondefense business grew to plan. New demands were now placed on his time and capital. He needed people, plant, space and operating capital. Finally, after resisting the obvious for ten years, he decided to seek capital in the public marketplace. Utilizing Stevens as his prime contact, Enders took Climax public in the bear market of 1972, collecting $4,000,000 in fresh public money in the process. He'd resisted a public offering of stock during the Sixties on principle and for the practical reasons of the bleak market outlook of the Seventies. But he had no choice and with an earning record that looked like the history of a great thoroughbred, Climax, immeasurably helped by the presence of Stevens on its board, became a public company. It was no exception to the market, however. The stock opened at 12 and promptly plunged to just under 7 within 2 months of the first trade that crossed the tape.

But Enders was now personally relieved. He approved the Little Black Box budget for $300,000, scrutinizing in detail every element of the itemized expenses, feeling a public trust now guided his decision-making process. This amount, he felt, was within the confines of what he thought was usable. There was little or no fat in the budget. The people on the project were dedicated to it. And the $300,000 would bring them so much closer to the touchdown.

Incredibly, the growth of Climax was paced by the Little Black Box. By the end of 1972, it had already cost Climax $1,000,000 from an initial $15,000. One thousand answer-back boxes were now complete awaiting shipment. Then fate played its ever-unbeatable trump card. Stevens, still a vigorous 76, dropped dead on the golf course.

Enders learned of Stevens' death on the evening television news. Shaken, he immediately flew to the West Coast to person-ally extend his condolences to Stevens' family. He decided to remain on the Coast for the funeral and services, which took place a week later. His personal grief beginning to abate, Enders began to wonder, as he walked along in the driving rain from the tiny private cemetery outside San Fransisco, just how Buy TV was now going to move into its final, crucial, on-site test without the driving passion of the old man who'd just been lowered into the earth.

He telephoned McBain from his hotel. He told his associate he could not fly back to the East until he had a better fix on who would be assuming the operation of the on-site test. He confessed, he said, to some dark premonitions. The following day, those fears assumed the hard shocking edge of reality. He met with Stevens' attorneys and learned that:

1] Stevens' fortune, publicly estimated at $50,000,000, had long ago been diverted into trusts foundations and annuities for his sons, daughters, and grandchildren. His late wife's fortune was considerably more modest, about $1,500,000, and it was initially the income from this which had provided the basic working capital for Buy TV.

2] Stevens had plunged the principal of his wife's estate into Buy TV as well. It was now virtually all gone.

3] Stevens had assembled his miniventure company as a limited-risk partnership and had brought in aged, former corporate cronies to give them all an interest in their twilight years.

4] The engineers, scientists, and marketing people he'd hired were all on "loan" from large corporations in which he was either a major stockholder (or his trusts were) or a member of the board. Their salaries had been continued by their companies and not paid by Stevens' venture group.

Enders sat listening, frozen in terror. He began to feel he'd been had. The following day, he visited the offices of Stevens Associated Television to confer with the executives. His impressions the previous day proved wrong. He'd not been "had" by Stevens. All of Stevens dealings had proven scrupulously honest. His bank connections were sound, his bills paid on time. His private correspondence with people in education, the arts, entertainment, and government bespoke a firm, unshakable conviction

in the feasability of his ideas. Even executives of his land development empire pointed out how Stevens' promotional campaigns
had been cited by state consumer affairs departments as exemplary of a candor rare in homesite promotion.

Vista Real was a moneymaker and that company itself had
sunk $40,000 into promoting the test to its residents. That was
all fine. But now that the old man was gone, the burning question
remained: *Who was in charge of Buy TV?*

An astonished Enders blinked at a mass of blank glances
and shrugged shoulders. Finally, one of the courtly old gentlemen cleared his throat and suggested, "Er, perhaps Mr. Enders,
your company would care to *buy* Buy TV? We wouldn't know
what to do with it even if the test succeeded."

A now-bewildered Enders attempted to thread his way logically through this insane tableau. What was there to buy? Stevens
Associated Television, Inc. had patents, some hardware, contracts with manufacturers, and a handful of wealthy old men who
really didn't care what happened to Buy TV so long as they had
a little fun keeping active.

Saddened by the pathetic, breaking man before them, the
old gentlemen whispered among themselves for several minutes
and decided to make Enders a token offer: They would give
Climax Buy TV in exchange for Climax shares, they would continue to lend the prestige of their names in the business community to the project, and would personally advance Climax half the
operating costs of the project for the following year.

A drowning Enders grabbed at the straw. The terms were
outlined:

1] 　The four old gentlemen would continue to operate
　　the program on behalf of the Stevens' estate. If the
　　program succeeded, Enders would get full control of
　　Buy TV. They also agreed the Stevens' estate would
　　have no claims on any income Buy TV might produce.
　　The attorneys for the estate agreed. Stevens' will had
　　provided for complete autonomy in operation and
　　disposal of Buy TV by his colleagues.

2] 　Climax would make another $100,000 its limit to the
　　end of the on-site test, and the four men would invest

$25,000 each to the company in exchange for Stevens
Associated stock, which, if the test succeeded, would
be converted to Climax stock. Stevens' executors
heartily agreed. They wanted nobody hurt.

3]   The four gentlemen agreed to use their personal
assets to collateralize loans up to $1,000,000 if needed
to complete the following phase of the project, which
was the extension of the test into 50,000 homes.

Enders returned to New York after a 5-week ordeal on the
West Coast. He ordered his Little Black Box team, which had
been suspended pending final arrangements, to get back to work.
He ordered his public relations people to turn on the big lights
at the Vista Real site with weekly bulletins on installation progress. Now what happened? What follows is a classic sequence in
most "little bit more" histories:

1]   The site installers suddenly hit water which had not
appeared on any of the geological surveys previously
used. Somebody forgot to check that the last survey
was 6 years old. Nobody expected water to materialize
in 6 years where it had not been for 6 million, but
neither did anybody stop to think that the original
survey had been commissioned by Stevens to a
student geology group as part of a personal pet
"Young Peoples" project. The report had been sent
to a professional geology firm who began preparations
for a site study using it only for general background.
Because Stevens had a vitriolic argument with one of
the geologists, he fired them, demanding they return
the original student survey. They did, but a secretary
had inadvertently placed the student report in
between the report-cover binders of the geological
firm, and it was mailed back in that form and filed.
Whenever it was pulled out from that time on, people
naturally assumed it had been conducted by the
professional firm when, in fact, it was the work of
students. Stevens had forgotten about it completely,
age having played this trick on his memory. The

presence of the water necessitated relocating a special large monitoring station and antenna system 3 miles away. Climax was required to dispatch a team of engineers to pitch in for a site study to determine the second-best location for the station. This added $25,000 to the cost.

2] The first entertainment offerings scheduled for the test had become ensnared in a jurisdictional dispute between the owners of certain entertainment properties. As time neared for the opening date, it began to look as if no entertainment, as had been lavishly promised the residents, would be available. A firm of lawyers specializing in these matters was retained and rendered a $12,500 bill after giving up on the case.

3] The costs of advertising and promotion originally budgeted at $30,000 ran closer to $45,000, adding an extra $15,000 to the costs.

4] The mail order company which had agreed to prepare and fulfill the merchandising part of the program backed away over internal disputes as to what kind of products would be offered. They too were a small, unknown company which had poured, "bit by bit," nearly $80,000 of their own money into the program. Their new company president, who was more concerned about getting the company back on its feet in its regular business, merely blue-pencilled a proposed allocation of $10,000 for the final phase. No contract anywhere bound them to deliver. Climax needed to find another merchandising company. Nobody had time to look. So Enders hired a man at $45,000 a year to find one. The man was a department store executive between jobs who left after 3 months to return to his field, bewildered by the whole atmosphere of electronics.

The always dispassionate, cool, logical Enders, facing what began to resemble a debacle, could no longer withstand the nervous tension. He finally suffered a nervous breakdown and was ordered to take complete bed rest for six weeks. During his recovery, he was barred by his doctors from receiving anything or sending anything to the office. So it was McBain, acting on his behalf during his illness, who faced the final crisis.

Another engineering study had revealed certain minor flaws in equipment during on-site testing. Another 5 months and another $65,000 would be required to solve the "minor flaws." It happened that the emergency had developed during the same week as a Climax board meeting. McBain authorized the go-ahead but, simultaneously, requested a routine audit of the entire project since its beginning just in case he was asked questions by the board. A day before the board meeting, a thin, five-page report was laid on his desk. McBain read it and on the last page where all expenses were tabulated, he simply couldn't believe his eyes.

The Little Black Box, since the first day 4 years ago when Enders had returned from the Coast with news of his chance meeting with Stevens, had cost the company a staggering total of $1,789,000. With budget projected forward, the project would top $2 million to move out of the first 1,000 home Villa Real test. And all this, for what Climax had always thought was a tiny piece of the giant Buy TV project.

McBain was flabbergasted. He'd known all along about the costs. He'd been at every meeting. His partner never spent a nickel without asking his advice. Where had it gone? It was always another $10,000 for this or $25,000 for that. Not wishing to lay down beside his partner, McBain retired to his weekend cottage to think things through. The following day, he returned and telephoned the West Coast, advising them he was on his way out.

The next afternoon, he held a meeting at the Stevens offices with the four old boys, the P.R. people, and the engineering people. He told them, in effect, that his company had laid nearly $2,000,000 into the project and he wanted to know how much everyone else had put in. The very accomodating old boys summoned the records. Stevens had gone for about the same amount. But no one else involved had gone so deep into the well. No one even close.

McBain faced up to the grisly facts:

1] Nobody had gypped Climax.

2] Nobody really cared, it seemed, one way or another, if
   Buy TV *ever* became anything. Everyone was,
   curiously, just going along—the same way Climax did
   —along for a frivolous and seemingly cheap ride.

3] Climax was caught, it seemed, in one of those
   inextricable, inexplicable, human conundrums—a
   drama without a hero, a catastrophe without a villain.
   There were no good guys to summon. There were no
   bad guys to blame. There was just the two million
   bucks down the drain. "How did we get ourselves in
   this goddamn mess?" McBain scribbled on a pad in
   his hotel room.

He'd been impressed at the meeting that day with the corporate P.R. man, Jeffreys, who had seemed to maintain a certain
skeptical good humor throughout the proceedings. McBain
asked Jeffreys to meet him for dinner that night for a chat. Here,
from the memory of one of the participants, is a reasonably
accurate narrative of the conversation that evening.

McBain: Bob, please level with me. Is this thing gonna
          go, or have we just been sucked in?

Jeffreys swallows his drink, lights his pipe, and cracks a
baleful smile.

Jeffreys: I'm sorry, Mac, but to me, it looks like, well,
           I don't know. Everybody means so goddamn well.
           The old man shoved over two million into it. But
           you see, I think the thing just is like an orphan.
           There's no daddy, no one with the patience and the
           energy to see it through. God knows the dough in-
           volved.

McBain: How'd the old man get involved?

Jeffreys sits erect from his slouch. He leans over, looking
directly at McBain.

Jeffreys: Look, Mac. Stevens was our client for twenty
           years; I knew the old guy only the last ten. But this
           much I did know. When they finally forced retire-
           ment on him he was like a wounded lion, whining
           around, nursing his ego, looking for something to
           do to show 'em all he still had the Stevens magic.

Then, Koler the engineer comes to him one day. He's got this pay TV idea, but the company won't let him develop it. It only takes a few lousy grand or so to buy some hardware. Couldn't the old man use his influence as honorary board chairman to get him a small appropriation?

McBain closed his eyes and drew deeply down on his cigarette. He'd heard it all before.

Jeffreys continued.

JEFFREYS: So the old man is intrigued. He invites Koler to his summer house in Oregon, and they keep talking about it during a weekend fishing trip. The old man loves the idea. Thinks it's sensational. A perfect outlet for his time and energy. One helluva toy.

McBAIN: A TOY! For chrissakes, a TOY! That goddamn toy cost us two million bucks!

JEFFREYS: You want my opinion, I'm giving it. Buy TV may be the next sliced bread or wheel or Second Coming of Christ. But I tell you, Mac, it was a toy to the old man and soon became a toy to his pals.

McBAIN: Why didn't anyone say anything! Why didn't his sons or daughters—

JEFFREYS: Cut it out, Mac—you know damn well why. Look, here's an old geezer, loaded with dough. Lots of things can happen. He can chase 16-year-old girls and give them ten grand to sit on his lap, or set up foundations for radical politicans on the lunatic extremes, or piss his money away dangerously. Stevens was a wholesome old guy. He lived to conquer new worlds; he had to continue as part of the scheme of things. So the family and all the people around him were happy he was in this thing. Gave him something good to do. His record was good. Made money on Vista Real. So they figured, like you, another hundred grand or so, what the hell did it mean when you had 50 million—

The conversation continued until midnight. But McBain heard very little of what Jeffreys said, his eyes now glassy with worry and drink. The next day, McBain flew to New York, resolved to bite the bullet.

He announced at the board meeting that due to unforeseen events and complexities in the test installation, the Buy TV project was being indefinitely postponed. To his surprise, there was general agreement on the board. Later, he realized why. Most of the money that had gone into Buy TV had been earned before the company was public—it belonged to Enders and to him. Why should the board care about the Little Black Box, after all?

At the end of the year, however, when Climax earnings were sharply down—actually due to a cyclical downturn in business and not the project—the board looked for an excuse to remove Enders and McBain. They found the Little Black Box audit and made it into a company scandal. Enders and McBain resigned under fire.

The new management administered the final dose which was to kill Climax Electronics. With the downturn in the economy and the cities starving for Federal aid, budgets for new electronic security equipment plunged, taking with it the sales of Climax. Its new management wildly sought government contracts, which were tough to get. Without Enders and McBain to guide it, the company fell deeper and deeper in debt until it was declared bankrupt.

An old Climax employee, now retired, still corresponds with Enders, who lives on a small, quiet farm in western Ireland. The old technician recently asked Enders to give his son some advice about a project relating to a revolutionary new burglar alarm. Enders advice was succinct:

> *Dear Ted,*
> *Your father has asked me to advise you about that burglar alarm system this cop wants to sell you cheap.*
> *Take it from a dummy who learned. You'll always be better off selling a bargain than buying one.*
> > *Sincerely,*
> > *Robert Enders*

AUTOPSY

The Climax story is like the notable tale of the bum who asked
for a dollar for a cup of coffee because, as he told the passer-by,
he was a big tipper. You'd probably help any reasonably gallant
panhandler with a dime. Maybe you'd even help ten. But the first
guy to lean on you for a buck would probably get a sneer. You
never feel anything a dime at a time.

As obvious a lesson as this story is, businessmen just don't
learn. Like Robert Enders, they never see themselves as others
see them. They get sucked in, dime by dime, because Enders, his
associates, and probably you, are just too human to pass up a
bargain. Sure, you can pinpoint errors Enders committed if you
reread his story. But were they really errors? Or were they good
judgments that backfired?

The origins of Enders' problems were his workable assumptions that $15,000 was little enough to invest to get a chunk of
the potential payout of the Stevens Buy TV scheme.

Enders didn't recall that bargains like the one offered by the
well-meaning Stevens simply do not exist in the real world of
business. We've all heard those mind-boggling stories about the
men who parlayed 50 bucks into 50 million. But we all should
understand that for every guy who bought the 10 acres of dust
that turned a gusher, there are 10,000 who bought emaciated
piglets in the poke. That's how people who sell bargains get rich.

While Enders had no palpable reason to carp at the odds
when Stevens first presented the Buy TV scheme to him, he
should have had dozens of reasons to suspect that 15,000 buying
a payout in millions was just a little bit too much luck a little too
fast. While certainly not a case to reject Stevens' offer, the sheer
odds of a payout like that should have brought Enders to a halt.
Timing was, to some degree, favorable. He was predisposed. He
was looking for something. But his search was too sudden a
departure from a proven success formula he himself had meticulously constructed. He'd built his business on sound ideas; quality well above competition, price integrity, small runs, prompt
delivery, and tender loving care of each order. Not everyone can
make that formula work. It takes a special breed of man. Having

mastered it, Enders was a fool to suddenly allow himself to get sucked into what was, by comparison, an innocent, fast-buck operation.

He didn't have the animal instincts, the gambler's dynamic, if you will, working for him. If he were a fast operator, he'd probably had sold off his part of the action for a profit or a loss in short order. But once he made the initial error, his tenacious, unwavering mentality would not let him quit. Each successive investment numbed him to the one just ahead. Once past the point of no return, the momentum swung heavily ahead, taking with it all reason to turn back. The only way Enders could have assured not getting overcommitted was by not committing dime one. What was the alternative?

Had Enders continued on his course without the sharp turn in Buy TV, he could have focused more intensely on the job at hand without bothersome diversion. We can only speculate as to the results. Perhaps he'd have sunk his money into something else. He was, however, a proven performer in his own little field, and whether it's a horse, a football team, or a company, most of the time, a chart player outperforms a longshotter.

You may well ask, What would have happened if Enders' small initial risk would have paid off? Longshots do pay off from time to time. Had Buy TV succeeded, Enders could have made $5,000,000. There is not a remote chance that he could have made nearly as much within the framework of his regular business.

Most gamblers who make it, however, roll high and fast. Few men have made fortunes by risking dribble by dribble; waging a company's resources bit by bit is dumb. Enders was not a big gambler; his plodding mind wasn't tuned to big movements of men and money. His business functioned like a finely tuned and precise Swiss watch, an extension of his own mind. In becoming enmeshed in Buy TV, he fell into the trap of lesser men who throw just a little bit more into the pot each time with wishful thinking.

Enders killed his business by playing with the delicate mechanism of the call of a beautiful bargain on a sunny shore. He lost his way, drop by drop by drop by drop.

8

Retail Roulette—The Error of Constant Change

> He is very foolish who aims at pleasing all the world and his father.
>
> —LaFontaine

P E R H A P S the most perplexing problem facing the manager or owner of a small business today is the recurring conflict between the company's necessity to maintain the contemporaneity of its products and services and its obligation to continue earning a profit on what it presumes to be its basic business.

We hear too many Gothic tales about companies flushed down the bowl because their managements failed to respond to the challenge of change. We listen to the bleeding souls of friends trapped in companies which resist change defiantly, pouting and sneering at the natural laws of small business survival. We don't hear enough, however, about the companies overzealous for change, overeager to prove just how *au courant*—how terribly space age—they are. These often become the most eerie horror stories of all.

It's tough to disagree about the blindness of companies whose clerks still sit perched on stools with visors, scribbling on foolscap with ball-point quills. In too many small outfits, however, change can become a full-time hobby resulting in confusion and waste, tragic losses of time, energy, resources, and momentum. An overrich diet of change can take its toll just as the incrustation of status quo can. And because too little has been said about caloric changes that cause commercial coronaries, we submit now, the story of The Medway Company.

James T. Medwick and Ansel Rodway, two first cousins, 25 and 27 respectively, quit the East Central Electric Company in

1905 to invest their small savings in a dry-goods store on the Main Street of Quentin, a surging industrial town amid the rolling hills of an East Central dairy district. To the city's population of 50,000, in 1905, there trickled, and then flooded, immigrants, pouring in from the Eastern metropolises and Europe itself, to man the unskilled jobs at the budding machine tool plants, steel mills and packing houses of Quentin.

But it was not from this burst of immigrant industrial masses that the Medway Dry Goods Store thrived, but from the growing middle and upper-middle classes of Quentin drawn from the offices at the mills, the professionals and businessmen, and the comfortable dairy farmers in the surrounding counties. Adjacent to Medway's was Levy's Dry Goods Store on Front Street which was mobbed with working-class housewives buying cheap muslins, cottons, and wools. Each store thrived in the measured way in which American retailing was nourished by growing prosperity and the mass distribution of consumer goods. By 1925, a new generation had grown up but Medway's remained an institution to one group and Levy's to another. Quentin and its surrounding suburbs now contained nearly 200,000 people and one either shopped at Levy's or one could afford to shop at Medway's, for both were now nearly fully stocked department stores, each having gobbled up nearly every store on its own original blockfront.

Medway's began pulling away. The steadily rising families from a 100-mile radius made twice-annual pilgrimages to Quentin for holiday shopping because Medway's was the only store in half the state which carried goods comparable in scope, style, and quality to the finest emporiums of Fifth Avenue or State Street.

While the Depression held Levy's in place, it became a spur to the continuing growth of Medway's which dominated the retail status of the entire state. In 1932, Medway's opened its first branch store in the posh new Highgate suburb east of the city. Levy's followed a year later but was forced to close within 6 months. Medway's remained healthy because, Depression or not, its customers had by now hardened into a "clientele" while Levy's now competed head-on with three other popular-priced department stores which had since opened in Quentin. A family which shopped at Medway's prior to the 1929 crash but could no longer afford it, continued shopping there anyway, on credit, to maintain that most curious of small-city, middle-class mores, "appearances."

So the Depression not only preserved Medway's status image, it nourished it. Cheap labor now made it possible for Medway's to create a whole new menu of Old World snob services. Lackeys in page uniforms held doors, carried packages to waiting cars, served milady a cool drink in summertime if she felt faint while trying on a corset a size too small. The lackey brigade swelled with refugees from the quiet mills and plants, thankful for jobs as pages, doormen, porters, or messengers. One cold morning in January 1936, the people in the old South Side awoke to what they saw as a divine apparition. Deliverance had come. The tall brick smokestacks of Quentin Steel #2 were belching out black smoke. By 10 A.M., the postman had brought the news. Q2 was hiring again.

The reopening of Quentin Steel #2 plant signaled the first stirring out of the darkness of the Depression. On that same day, old Hyman Levy, the picture of conservatism, black-suited, vested, and puffing a cigarette from a silver holder, met his old friend, James T. Medwick, at Wilson's Garage while their chauffeurs gassed up.

Hyman pointed out what a brilliant winter day it was. Jim agreed. Hyman pointed out what a wonderful thing it was that Quentin Steel #2 was back working at 50 % capacity. Jim agreed. Hyman advanced the opinion that business would now regenerate and that Levy's would be facing the greatest growth in its history. Jim hoped it would be the case for his old friend. Then Hyman faced Jim directly. "Jim, I need your prime location on Main. I'm willing to pay. Why don't you move the store further uptown to where the other better trade have gone, and sell me your property? Sooner or later, I'm going to dominate downtown anyway. I'll pay you a handsome profit."

Jim Medwick gracefully laughed off Hyman's suggestion as hyperbole. But that evening, as he sat carving the dinner roast at a family party, his son, Charles Medwick, was not so convinced Levy's offer was funny at all.

Charles was now 35. He was preparing to assume the presidency of the store that year. He was tentative about his father's merchandising policies, successful though they were in raising Medway's to a 200,000-square-foot operation of four floors from a small dry-goods store. He worried about the clear exercise of logic Hyman Levy had suggested to his father. Downtown was becoming a popular-priced center. Ten blocks north was where all the private better shops now clustered. Scruffy characters and shabby stores had sprouted up along the side streets adjacent to Main. The following day at the store, Charles told his father he oughtn't have dismissed Levy's offer as a joke. With the Depression corner turned, old Hyman may indeed have had a point.

Jim listened patiently to his son. Then he called Charles to his office window. Father and son watched as an ancient man in a spiffy Medway's porter's uniform gracefully led a frail dowager queen out of the store and into her waiting limousine carrying ten large boxes bearing the familiar, blue, Medway, crinoline lady logo.

"See that, Charlie, old Mrs. Hiram Stix Fox. What she spends here on a weekday, fifty of Hyman's customers don't spend in a month. Holding that customer down there is our business, and she'll come and continue to come to wherever we are. Let Levy's hog all the millworkers' wives he wants. He's good at it. And millworkers' wives are his business."

Charles was not entirely convinced.

"There's a helluva lot more mill wives than Mrs. Hiram Foxes. And besides, she and all her kind must be a hundred years old now. What do we do in ten years?"

"Worry not, my son," said Jim smiling, "as long as there's people on God's little earth, there's gonna be Mrs. Hiram Foxes, and what's so great is that we don't need millions of them to keep Medway's making money."

Charles shrugged his resignation to his father's judgment. But he continued to wonder.

For a good many years afterward, events appeared to bear out old Jim's viewpoint. He passed away in 1938, in what was for Medway's a record year in sales and profits. Still slightly skeptical, but no less convinced of his father's wisdom, Charles Medwick continued a strong policy of status and quality until by the outbreak of World War II, Medway's was the match of any fine speciality department store in any big city in America. Charles had introduced the ladies of Quentin to French couture, English bone china in a dazzling assortment of patterns, fine British woolens, and hand-carved toys. When war came to Quentin, Jim Medwick's policy was not only sound business, it began to look like downright prophecy.

With the factories, plants, and foundries of Quentin pounding away for the war effort two- and three- shift days, a mass of new families of income and influence poured into Medway's, money bulging in their pockets, ready to buy and buy heavily anything that Medway's had to sell.

But the war economy had another, less salubrious, effect on Medway's than the rising register tapes.

Their lackey brigade disappeared. The thousands of new factory jobs created by the wartime economy depleted Medway's ranks of able-bodied porters and pages fast. Anyone who could walk, talk, write, or spit in a straight line was marched into the waiting plants to the strains of "Praise the Lord and Pass the Ammunition," and a Friday check with overtime that was more than he'd earned toadying for tips at Medway's in a month.

No longer serfs, these people and the thousands upon thousands whom the war had uplifted into real live consumers, now flooded into Levy's, necessitating an almost monthly extension of the old bargain store into every shop, loft, and office building ground floor along Front Street. Levy's now opened a second store to the west of the city, where the new, working-class blacks, released from misery as sharecroppers in the South, began to settle.

This continued expansion and bustling prosperity of both Medway's and Levy's suddenly slowed around 1950. One bright May morning in that year, Charles Medwick opened his newspaper and read with anxiety the following item:

JASPER'S TO OPEN FIRST
NEW STORE SINCE DEPRESSION.
QUENTIN BRANCH TO OPEN
THIS FALL

CAPITOL CITY. Jasper & Company, the state's oldest department store, will open its first branch store outside the state capital in Quentin this fall. The new

branch store is also the first Jasper's branch to be
opened since 1931.
    Marion J. Jasper, Jr., Chairman of the posh
chain, said: "This move is a natural outgrowth of our
continuing effort to service the discriminating, high-
income families of our state."

Rumors of Jasper's invading Quentin had flown past
Charles' ears for ten years. He paid little attention to them when,
after the war, nothing happened as he'd presumed. He had, by
then, assumed all that would ever come of the rumors was conversation in the soft goods showrooms of New York's Seventh
Avenue. Charles immediately called his friends in local real estate
circles to find out just where the Jasper's branch would open. His
own private guess had always been uptown on Fifteenth Street,
where all the smart ladies' dress stores had long ago clustered.
He was right, but he hadn't guessed anything about the background of the move.

He learned that Jasper's move into Quentin was the result
of an agreement in principle for Levy's to purchase 60% of Jasper's. Jim Medwick had not told his son the full story of Hyman
Levy's original offer. He now learned from Hyman and his son-
in-law, Kenneth Demberg, who was going to run Jasper's, that
Hyman had not only offered to buy the property in which Medway's was housed but the business itself. What Hyman Levy
wanted that day in the garage was not only a store, he wanted a
foothold into the better retailing market. Having been politely
spurned by Jim, he pressed his suit with Marion Jasper and finally
convinced him that the combined financial power of Levy's and
the status leverage of Jasper's could produce a formidable assault
on Medway's iron grip on Quentin's carriage trade. Hyman Levy
had begun acquiring property uptown years ago, and the parcels
he now owned were to be assembled into a four-acre site at the
center of which was the fine, old, neo-Grecian, five-story Farmer's building which would house Jasper's.

Jasper's opened that September less than a mile away from
Medway's. Unfortunately, Charles Medwick did not enjoy the
same personal rapport with Kenneth Demberg that his father had
with Hyman, so Demberg didn't have the slightest interest in ever

repeating his father-in-law's offer. Demberg relished the competitive battle, and with both men now girded for combat, Demberg presented the first challenge.

Medwick's merchandising vice president rushed into Charles' office the day Jasper's opened flushed in panic. "The goddamn place is a movie set, Charlie. You can't believe the money they must have poured into that renovation. Plexiglass staircases, cathedral ceilings, chandeliers with three hundred bulbs, leather walls; it's totally devastating. The women are absolutely drunk."

Demberg had spared nothing. Jasper's had a plush beauty parlor, a charming restaurant decorated like a quaint Breton cafe, make-up demonstrations, fashion shows, and strolling guitarists playing requests. There was a White Carnation Shopping Service for men who couldn't think of what to get their wives for anniversaries and birthdays, a fully staffed nursery that attended to the kiddies while milady shopped, and a pool and gymnasium in a health club in the basement which was decorated like a Florida hotel of the era. Demberg had enticed every famous designer and clothing house to send representatives to help women with their fall wardrobes. Jasper's opening was a true event, and its effect on Medway's sales that week was devastating. Medway's was off 15%.

Charles tried to remain calm. He wisely remembered that Jasper's would have to prove itself in the face of the 45 years of tradition and habit which was the mark of Quentin's upper-middle class. Jasper's would not be the first out-of-town retailer to invade Quentin with great excitement and turn tail a year later, done in by the indomitable loyalties of all the Mrs. Hiram Foxes old Jim had always counted on.

But Charles could not wait. He picked up the gauntlet and came thundering right back at Demberg. He decided the best parry was a similar display of retailing lightworks. October 27 was proclaimed Founder's Day (October 27, 1905 was the day old Jim and his cousin had signed the lease on their original store). Charles created a magnificent panorama of Quentin's past interwoven with appearances of famous Quentin native sons and daughters, politicians, and show folk all dressed in turn-of-the-century garb. There was an import bazaar, ten fashion shows, a home decorating extravaganza, and television coverage of a Founder's Day Parade. A day before Halloween, Medway's distributed 5,000 surprise packages of candy and toys to the city's neediest children. Charles offered an unprecedented "Day at the Medwicks' "—a magnificent luncheon, tour, and carriage ride around his country estate out of town—to anyone opening a new charge account. This event alone brought 350 new accounts into the store—an all-time record.

Underlying this explosion of events, of course, was the shrewd, but not very subtle, reminder that Medway's had been around Quentin over 45 years and Jasper's was just a snotnose upstart from the state capital.

The results were terrific. Shoppers flooded into Medway's and "rediscovered" the charms of the institution. Sales surged. Now both Charles and Demberg battered each other head-on with events, sales, and show business. This war of the Barnums ended in a stalemate. When the tinsel cleared, Jasper's was still standing, its cash registers ringing merrily away; Medway's holding firm, not run an inch off its turf. Charles Medwick was unhappy. In this kind of stalemate, he reasoned, he had to be the loser.

Less than a year later, events grimly unfolded as Charles had foretold. Medway's gross sales slipped at the close of the fiscal year and, for the first time in the company's 46-year history, earnings were flat. Charles Medwick, now frightened, determined on a bold counterattack. If show business retailing was what the citizens of Quentin's upper classes wanted, that's what he'd give them. He left Quentin and embarked on a month-long trip around the nation visiting the upper-strata department stores, pruning for ideas and fishing for people to execute them. He returned to Quentin invigorated and ready to copy what he'd seen.

An army of workmen now descended upon Medway's, gutting its interior like a flash fire. All four floors were refixtured with slick glass and walnut showcases. Dozens of old blue-veined ladies were sent out to pasture and replaced with corn-silk-haired young ladies from Quentin's best families. Import dress, sportswear, and shoe departments were added and the last of the lackeys were put out to pension. But Charles Medwick's biggest bet was on his brand new "Center Sophisticate" department which sprawled across half the second floor. Center Sophisticate was like most departmental names in retail stores—a euphemism. It was, in reality, a snazzy way of introducing more moderately priced, higher-styled merchandise to appeal to younger women. This new department was the expensive centerpiece of Charles Medwick's hunch that what Medway's needed was a quick injection of youth. Predictably, this department attracted customers drawn from a broader economic spectrum. Young working women who would have never considered crossing the revolving-door entrance before, now crowded into Medway's during sale days in the Center Sophisticate department, grabbing up the quality things at great prices.

Medway's shocked old blue bloods began trickling away in protest, watching in terrified disbelief as typists, clerks, and movie cashiers walked in and out of Medway's, carrying blue shopping bags with the crinoline lady printed on them.

The old guard trickled away by the dozens at first and then by the hundreds, fleeing uptown to Jasper's and to the barks of smart little shops now lining the posh streets from Fifteenth north. Jasper's held firm its superstylish image, despite some reservations that some of Demberg's executives had about all the ladies fleeing from Medway's only to find the same thing at Jasper's. But Demberg knew little old ladies better than most. His mother was archetypical of the breed, having come from a merchant family that had settled in Quentin in the 1850's. Demberg figured the essential thing was to preserve Jasper's snob image by keeping price brackets high and famous style names prominent. Then with superb retail cunning, Demberg slowly inveigled the Medway refugees into his net by exercising strong style leadership; if Jaspers said it was right, it was right. Tradition was fine, but it was only one point of view.

The young married women, already a solid Jasper's phalanx, failed to be enticed by Medway's attempts at updating the store and snapping up the merchandise mix. A Jasper's woman was a very predictable middle-class lady. She wanted the best, but she wanted to know that her contemporaries in New York, Chicago, and Los Angeles were wearing the same things.

The net result on Charles' attempt to swing Medway's into

the twentieth century was a fizzle. But that wasn't his only problem. The attack from Jasper's barely parried, Charles Medwick
now faced another foray into his domain, from—of all places—
Levy's.

Levy's, continuing its 40-year tradition of marketing directly to lower end of the middle class, utilized the style-setting
brains which had been included in the package which came with
Jasper's and now opened a large "Talk of The Town Shop" in
which the same high-styled merchandise shown at Jasper's and
Medway's was copied at popular prices. Levy's thrust into style
was instantly successful. Jasper's remained unruffled, and if they
were ruffled, it wouldn't matter. All the shekels were now pouring
into the same corporate till. It was Medway's, of course, which
absorbed the shock by watching its midrange Center Sophisticate
department wilt.

So now, Medway's had been caught in an impossible
squeeze play. Jasper's, with no great image to preserve, willingly
accepted anyone who wanted quality and would stretch to afford
it and Levy's quickly weaned away Medway's lower-end customers with their bargain-priced copies of famous originals. Distressed by this crunch, Charles Medwick felt the time had come
to out-Jasper Jasper's. Once again, he went out across the land
seeking an idea or a person.

Charles' trip to New York produced a spectacular coup. He
enticed Stacy Wynne, president of the prestigious Tower &
Weekes of New York's 57th Street, to move westward into Quentin and assume the presidency of Medway's. Mrs. Wynne had a
well-deserved reputation for brilliance as well as for being an
incarnation of the toughest lady sonofabitch who ever played in
a Rosalind Russell movie.

She was pure Eastern Establishment. Forty-fivish, dynamic,
and superintelligent, she boasted friends and contacts among the
most accomplished people on the planet. Not only fashion lead-
ers but world-famous political people, entertainers, artists, writ-
ers, and musicians had followed her from her beginnings in her
own store in Philadelphia fifteen years before through her years
at Tower & Weekes as the all-powerful dynamo of style, good
taste, and luxury living. A continuing pressure from the conglomerate which now owned Tower & Weekes had aroused her pique.

Charles ambled along hungrily at the right time. She figured a brief respite in the calm of mid-America might be a good prescription. So in she came, dragging her legend behind.

It was now the beginning of 1958, and Quentin's first luxury apartment house was rising beside a magnificent bend in the White River. Stacy rented the penthouse, elbowing out the Chairman of the Quentin National Trust Company in the process. She had Charles Medwick pony up over $75,000 to have it furnished by a prominent New York decorator and took the battle of rags to the social pages of Quentin's two daily newspapers.

She lavished a literal blitzkrieg of cocktail parties, fashion luncheons, dinner parties, and cultural bashes upon the delighted social set of Quentin. She sought to create a glitter about herself that she knew would rub off on the store. She succeeded handsomely. Medway's slightly worn and slightly tarnished image was refreshed, polished, and refocused. Old customers slowly ebbed back. The late '50s college crowd, no longer automatic State U. enrollees, brought back from the East, South, and West a heightened sense of style and pace. Stacy Wynne caught that mood right, made certain Medway's was well stocked with these goods, and sales began once again to climb.

With this quick success, Stacy Wynne found her feet fast and felt strong enough to recommend another major renovation. She wanted Medway's to forget the old bluestockings and the rising middle classes which were shifting from Levy's into Jasper's. She wanted the young and hip people of metropolitan Quentin, and to get them Medway's had to look young.

Medway's College Humor Fashion Ball based on a Roaring Twenties theme during mid-August of 1958, was such a smash that all Quentin cheered it in the press, on television, and on women's morning radio talk shows. Sales moved briskly upward, every customer in the city enchanted by the sparkling colors and ingenious, easy casuality of the new Medway's interior. Departments servicing middle-aged groups were stripped to tiny corners. Medway's famous gift department, where for generations proper young ladies had bought engagement gifts of prissy little creamers for each other, disappeared.

Stacy Wynne bounced the remaining Old Guard clerks and restaffed the advertising and publicity departments with the best talent she could wean away from top Chicago stores. Sensing Medway's had finally struck the vein of gold, both Levy's and Jasper's responded by expanding their own junior departments. But now, when all the old antagonists thought they could lean back, lick their financial wounds, and make a few bucks, a new, powerful force from the West rolled across the land and reached Quentin; it was called the boutique.

Along a row of quaint old stores built during the Twenties in the plush Highgate suburb, a new, vigorous type of retail store began assuming the expired leases of musty bookstores and French cleaners. The most popular of these new boutiques was Jacky's.

Jacky's specialized in the young female consumer like no other store anywhere within 500 miles of Quentin. It didn't just sell merchandise; it sold ideas. Service was not with a smile but with vintage rock-and-roll Muzak pumped in through a blasting high-fidelity unit. Jacky's expanded rapidly because it was not just a place to shop; it was a place to *be*. The ownership didn't take the familiar route in retailing success either. Instead of buying out leases and moving into bigger and bigger stores, Jacky's began opening new stores like hamburger stands. By 1959, there were six Jacky's planted all over the affluent and semiaffluent neighborhoods of Quentin. How did these six little shops threaten the exciting new creation of big city genius Stacy Wynne?

It was not Jacky's itself that threatened Medway's halting rebirth, but what Jacky's represented. A new question arose: Was it an entirely sound idea to base the entire future of a major department store on servicing a market better handled by dozens of smaller independent outlets?

Many of Medway's key merchandising people began pressing that question into meetings with Charles and Stacy Wynne. Among the most relentless interrogators at these meetings was Charles Medwick's eldest son, George, a recent arrival from The Wharton Business School at the University of Pennsylvania. George had now entered the family business as a third-generation Medwick growing uneasy about the future stability of his legacy.

George's uncertainties were based on two things. First was the fact that his girl friend and her girl friends shopped almost exclusively at Jacky's, despite the fact that George's girl, at least, could have taken anything she wanted from Medway's either free or at wholesale.

Second, George was a bit of a skeptic about Stacy Wynne. He suspected her consciousness had stopped dead somewhere between 1949 and 1956. He dubbed her "Joan Crawfoot" in private and carped constantly to his father about his misgivings. Charles rebuffed George, proudly pointing to the steadily rising sales figures the store had enjoyed since Stacy's arrival. He also pointed out that George knew nothing about the business and until he did, he'd best shut his trap. To learn a few things, he assigned George to work directly with Stacy as her operating assistant.

George began his real education in retailing under Stacy Wynne's baleful glare. She told George that her conversion of the store to a "young place" was merely a temporary stopgap to arrest the slide in sales. Her longer-range master plan was to capture them while they were young so that, when they married and raised families, they'd come to Medway's for babies' and children's clothes, house furnishings, and all their husbands' clothes. It was indeed a long-range plan, but after the gyrations that nearly brought Medway's to ruin before, she felt the compelling necessity to retrench into a small market segment, survive profitably, and expand to the original wider base when overall operations improved.

George Medwick bought Stacy Wynne's views for awhile. It bothered him somewhere although he couldn't pinpoint how. His head was swirling with ideas—in a raging mood to revolt, to change the world, and to get moving. So old Joan Crawfoot continued puffing her long cigarettes and pacing about her office worrying about the next month's sale items while George Medwick stewed and his father waited.

The 1960 Christmas season was a disappointment. This was partly due to economic factors, partly due to misplaced, old outmoded notions about the value of "events" in the mind of Stacy Wynne, and partly due to the growing power of smaller stores on Medway's perimeter. George Medwick used the occasion to once again importune his father about his very expensive, fading movie star.

Shaken by the lackluster 1960 fiscal results, Charles Medwick began to listen. This year would be the first year in the 55-year history of the store that the figures on the bottom line were red. What plans did Mrs. Wynne now have? How did she suppose she was going to reverse the trend? Where was the bottom line?

Charles called Stacy Wynne into his office one bright January morning. He gallantly expressed confidence in her but asked whether she could give him an insight into her 1961 plans earlier this year. Last year's loss, although miniscule in dollar terms, had badly shaken the family directors.

The old pro proudly laid her plans before her boss, right on the spot, nothing written down, straight from her shoulder pads, so to speak. She pointed out that, while she had originally hoped to achieve more volume in 1960, she was immensely pleased that store operations were slimmer and morale higher than it had been in a decade. New charge accounts were moving to record highs each month. Mailings drew more response each month. But most of all, she felt the image of Medway's was now firmly refixed in the Quentin psyche and that 1961 would show all this in record sales and profits.

Her final fillip was a shrewd explanation as to why she thought the ending figures showed a loss. She'd had to decide whether to close out a large collection of coats and suits early that previous fall to gain the liquidity she felt she wanted her buyers to have for Spring 1961 or hold the merchandise, clogging up the lines of buying availability until it turned. She decided she wanted her buyers to have "big pencils" for the Spring 1961 merchandise because it was exciting. So she moved out to markdowns to liberate monies. The $24,500 loss shown on the company's books was essentially the loss from that drastic markdown. She promised they'd make it up five times that Spring.

Charles Medwick still failed to perceive how so many healthy signs as she had explained them could produce a loss. He understood the reasons, of course, but he couldn't help expressing his disappointment over the loss in fiscal 1960 and, more critically, the shortfall of over $400,000 on targeted sales volume.

Stacy Wynne's large, gray eyes burned with scornful anger. She was a woman who had battled toe to toe with America's most prominent retailers and merchants. She would not accept even a gentle rebuff from a small-timer like Charles Medwick. She stood up from her chair and looked directly at Charles.

"If you can't see what I am talking about, Charles, then either your perception level has sunk below sea level, or you are as dumb as I thought you might have been when I first met you in New York." An astonished Charles Medwick flushed in embarrassed confusion. She extended her hand, said a courteous good-bye, and left Quentin that afternoon for the home of a movie producer friend in Palm Springs, California.

Charles Medwick's inner torment continued, nearly 30 years after it began when his father's refusal to sell out to Levy bothered him. The following morning, he announced Stacy Wynne's resignation with deep regret and placed himself in the presidency again until his son, George, accumulated the necessary experience.

George Medwick, heir apparent, decided to learn the retail business fast; he promptly left Quentin, seeking solutions for the problems of Medway's thousands of miles away. His "fact-finding mission," which was to last 6 weeks, stretched nicely into nearly 2 years. He traveled throughout the United States and then on to Europe to see what he could see, drink what he could drink, and deflower what he could deflower. He finally returned in 1963, his father about $100,000 poorer for the trouble, with a staggering, new idea: The department store was dead. Long live the discount house!

During his travels, George had actually worked for 5 weeks at a leading discount store in New York. He saw firsthand how discounting name brands on big-ticket general merchandise drew massive crowds and turned stupefying sums of volume. He could never forget, he told his father, those maddening crowds on Saturday mornings fighting their way into the store, pushing and shoving like stampeding animals, scooping up ten or fifteen pairs of socks at a clip, two radios, six folding beach chairs. Sating what seemed an unquenchable thirst for bargains was, in George's view, what the future of American retailing was all about.

George's case was sound. The discounters were mopping up the country in the early Sixties. They elbowed their way into prime downtown areas, pushing hard against entrenched old retail institutions and sending them all to run for cover, shell-shocked in disbelief at the prices these upstarts were selling merchandise for. During George's absence, his father had struggled with three different approaches to stem the hemorrhaging sales of Medway's. None of his policies had worked. His desperate mind was now disposed to anything.

Jasper's had all but sucked up the carriage trade, Levy's stood firmly battling the discounters popping up around its heels, and the poor, hapless Medway's was once again stuck in the middle. All dressed up and no place to go. After 58 years in business, Medway's had no face, no place in the scheme of a great American city.

At the emergency meeting of the family board called by his faltering father, George presented his case to the assembled Rodways and Medwicks who'd flown in for the occasion. They listened intently to George's plan to change the face of Medway's once again, this time to the concept of a "quality discount store" where not just names but great name brands would be discounted at "ridiculously low prices." The family listened with intense interest and voted overwhelmingly for George's plan. Even old Uncle Izak B. Medwick, nearing 85, pulled George to the side confessing that he, himself, a man reputed to be worth nearly $5 million in Telephone stock alone, shopped almost exclusively in discount stores. George was gratified. But he didn't hear another, perhaps more vital, comment from Uncle Ray, a prominent civil engineer. "I really voted in favor of George's plan," he told a Rodway in the elevator, "because this just has got to be the end. Those silly bastards have tried everything else. Maybe a stupid ploy like this will close the store down and we can sell the property to the downtown developers and finally make a big dollar."

George Medwick set about his task with religious fervor. He turned over five capital-hungry departments to lessees and extracted in exchange mercilessly high rents and fat percentages of the gross. He ripped out the entire ground floor and concocted a "Discovery" department, which featured a different assortment of imports each week displayed in great heaps; there were teak buckets from India, glass lamps from Italy, salt shakers from Finland, silver plates from Mexico, knit pants from England.

Discovery moved the goods, but not to Medway's regular

clientele. They all remained outside, terrified by the crush of steel mill workers and payroll clerks who mobbed in, grabbing up the buys. But George had no illusions about Medway's past as the Grand Dame of Quentin retail stores. He broke the store down into basics and changed the advertising to straightforward price-cutting borax, pushing ahead with bold inventory purchases on raw nerve and ringing registers.

George succeeded. Medway's was Quentin's first home-grown discount store of any consequence. Sales and profits rose, and it was generally conceded by the business community at large that the brash young Medwick had finally, and ironically, turned the empty silk purse into a very profitable sow's ear.

George rushed expansion throughout the middle-class sub-urbs that now ringed the city. By 1966, Medway's Value Centers had 8 stores doing a $10,000,000 annual volume. George flew to Europe, and with increasing frequency, to the great emporiums of the Far East, grabbing enormous quantities of import copies of successful originals he'd discounted. Again the magic worked; he was making money and volume shot past $12,000,000.

It finally seemed as though Medway's long, dark struggle with its image and corporate ego was over, dead and buried beneath a swelling corporate treasury. But it was not to be. Once again, that complex, congenital Medwick mechanism tripped and now attacked Medway's at the unluckiest of all possible times.

Super-Targeteer, a national discount chain, moved into Quentin. The giant discounter ironically took over the quarters of Levy's, which had since moved uptown into Jasper's old building (Jasper's having fled to the suburbs). The aggressive new team at Super began tearing Medway's apart like a high school biology student dissects his fifth frog.

They outspecialed Medway's on everything in a toe-to-toe confrontation. If Medway's ran Italian glassware at 10% off list, Super turned up with Hong Kong knockoffs of the Italian stuff at 50% under Medway's price. If Medway's ran electric razors 15% off list, Super gave them away at cost.

Once again, Medway's survival was challenged. Sales and profits lagged badly for 1967. Levy's and Jasper's were thriving merely by moving to where their well-developed customer base had moved. Medway's now stood helplessly again, rooted in the decaying downtown district, a discount operation being out-discounted by a lowball, shlock bargain store. George's choice was now to slug it out with Super or try to wait out the storm. Characteristically, he chose neither.

The audacious George spectacularly threw the entire business community of Quentin into frozen disbelief when instead of selling the property and closing the store and at a monstrous profit, he announced that Medway's was abandoning the discount field because of "price deterioration" and "reentering the quality retailing market that is our heritage and birthright." The family was outraged. Those who didn't think George was insane saw him as pathetic. But Quentin had come to expect these gyrations from the Medwicks, so everyone decided to stop clucking and watch the fun.

Once more, the long, white tarpaulins rolled down Medway's windows. Once again, the long lines of painters, carpenters, electricians, and decorators filed into the store while a now-amused public awaited the results. But this time, halfway through the great restoration, work suddenly stopped cold.

It seems that George had received an epiphany during one restless night, a manifestation promising the salvation of Medway's. He wanted the capital restoration budget changed to include a magnificent penthouse restaurant on the roof of the store which would rotate, offering the diners a magnificent view of the city's smokestacks at night. The new restaurant would add a minimum of $150,000 to the cost of one floor, and the builders were already estimating that the renovation would run over budget by at least another $300,000.

The family met in secret and rebelled, demanding George's resignation. They voted that the store be closed and sold to the City Development Corporation as a site for a new office tower.

So Medway's finally closed, a Quentin tradition ended.

Was it a victim of the times? Hardly. Jasper's survived and thrived in the same time. Levy's took a few blows, but absorbed them and remained sound.

A victim of circumstances? Perhaps. But one had to be blind not to see what was going on around the store.

What then? Medway's was a victim of many things, but most of all, it changed itself to death.

AUTOPSY

The idea that a business, large or small, in order to survive the vicissitudes of time and circumstance, must submit itself to a periodic change or checkup is a sound one. If we fail to recognize that basic truth, we are casting our lot with all the assorted idiots of history who refused to believe that the world was round, who thought Copernicus was a lunatic, and who classified Edison as a dreamer.

Life itself is change, is it not? One passes through childhood, adolescence, maturity, and old age. Unlike a person, however, a business does not necessarily have to die, even if its owners or managers set out to kill it.

We make no case here for blind truculence in a business that is gasping for change. Overcaution is often the worst policy in certain crisis situations. We'd like to make something of a case, however, for sometimes staying put.

The history of Medway's dramatically illustrates the phenomenon of swiveling and whirling which has characterized the policy decisions of too many small businesses in the United States. All too many guys spend too much precious time bobbing back and forth and too little time staying where they are, examining their options in a pinch situation and acting on the facts as they are.

Perhaps if you work for a company whose owners gyrate too, you may feel comforted by the fact that they might not be quite as dumb as Charles Medwick and his son, George, seemed to be. Take no solace. Charles and George were no dummies. They were, in fact, pretty bright guys. Their problem lay in their unshaken conviction that change for the sake of change was the only curative to a challenging situation.

The Medwicks could not decide what they wanted to be. They wanted success badly. They wanted survival badly. Who doesn't? To do that, however, they sacrificed their own clearmindedness about what they were in business to do. The schizoid behavior of store management kept consumers confused. Every store needs a reason to be. In retailing, a business can survive on a single product or service to which consumers respond with consistency. I know a man who runs a delicatessen with very ordinary products. But his potato salad is very special and people travel 15 miles out of their way to stock up on it—5 pounds at a time. People buy his stringy roast beef and his vinegary cole slaw and lousy brand of ice cream because his potato salad draws them to his store. He won't change anything he does. He is stubborn. Why? Because his store is a gold mine.

Their early start gave the Medway's people an entrenched position; They could have ruled retailing in Quentin. They chose, instead, to react to the arrival of their first real competition by trying to become something they were not. Medway's was a stuffy, old-fashioned, quality retail store. Their customers needed leadership in taste, not me-tooism. The idea was not to battle Jasper's for the trade they were losing, but merely to hold the trade they had until the first blush of novelty faded from Jasper's as it fades from every store. By seesawing back and forth between a quality store, a middle-line store, and a discount operation, they chose to fight on the other guy's grounds, not their own. This is a classical case in retailing blunders. One can't fight competitors on areas of competitive strength and come out intact.

Having stressed the quality and purity of the Medway's name for so long, they could not have endeared themselves to their own snobby customers by turning their store into a broader market. Stacy Wynne sensed this. But she also understood, as Charles had years before, that no retail store in the area could survive dependent on the handful of Mrs. Hiram Stix Foxes alone. She was a hard-headed, practical-minded merchant, and she knew she could draw Quentin's new generation of upper and middle classes into one larger, tight group by imposing a strong, highly focused, central image of young fashion leadership in Medway's which could not but help the store regain its dominant position in town. But the Medwicks were blind to her plans. They felt piqued and abandoned by their customers when Jasper's challenged, and they reacted with blind emotion instead of common sense. The Medwicks substituted money and frantic boldness for an admittedly less titillating plod forward on an established route to success which Stacy Wynne so clearly saw.

Once having decided that change was their basic reaction to

crisis, there was no helping the Medwicks. Each subsequent gyra-
tion only reinforced the inevitability of the eventual outcome.
Even the fleeting success of Medway's in the discount field dem-
onstrated the point that change can often buy short-term success,
but when it's the wrong change for the wrong reasons, its just
piling a second mortgage on a grim future.

A man whom I respect immensely as a businessman told me
that customers teach a man more about his business than suppliers, consultants, executives, and clerks, anyone. The educative
process is cheap and disarmingly simple. Yet you'd be shocked
how few businessmen learn.

1]   If your company is known for good deliveries and a
      few customers begin to complain, it means your
      deliveries are probably deteriorating. Most won't
      complain because you've a reputation for good
      delivery. If you don't take fast action to maintain your
      reputation, you won't have it to save.

2]   If your product line gets dull, your customers will
      quickly forget the stiffs you sold them but still buy
      from you because they will always harbor the hope
      that you will score again, the way you did five years
      ago, with another biggie. Don't look for another
      product line—see what's wrong with yours.

3]   If your prices rise too high and no one complains, it's
      not because your customers have accepted things
      sitting down. It's because your prices have probably
      been pretty fair in the past and they're understanding.
      But it's no signal for you to keep going. Remember,
      your image as a reasonably priced supplier is worth
      ten times the gold of the yield of a price rise. If
      you've established your business on price, let it grow
      on price. There are hundreds of stupid men running
      around the United States telling businessmen that
      there is something morally reprehensible about being
      a "price operation." Baloney. There's nothing wrong
      with being a price operator. Letting someone come in
      and sell you a suitcase full of dreams about the profits
      waiting for you with one little 5% price increase is

tantamount to suicide. If you have a healthy business, making a profit satisfactory to you and your family, screw the soothsayers. If you're smart enough to sell price, SELL IT. Don't be ashamed of it, like Medway's was ashamed of whatever image it created the year before. *Reinforce it and promote it.*

On the other hand, if you sell quality and not price, do the same. There is equally nothing morally reprehensible about getting a classical buck for a good product. Let the world know that you are selling the real stuff. If they want cheapie versions, let them buy them. When they're hungry, they can eat hamburgers. When they want to dine, let them come to your place for steak.

AUTOPSY

The autopsy findings of Medway's are that it died because it refused to understand that a business, like a person, must be true to itself to survive happily in a competitive world. Anyone who changes his personality every few days just to be loved is in for a peck of emotional problems. But a man, who is what he is and makes no bones about it, will survive because his head will be screwed on straight and he'll deal with crisis by reason.

If you're going to gamble with success, don't throw away your luck on pennies.

9

The Milky Way—The Fine Art of Self-Deception

D O E S a man who steals from his own business rob anyone but himself and the Internal Revenue Service? Is there such a thing in moral or natural law as stealing from oneself?

These two questions could take a philosopher a lifetime to answer. But if we assume, for the sake of rhetorical convenience, that stealing from one's own business is still stealing, we can state that the act of milking one's own business is probably the most pervasive and popular form of crime in America. Birds do it. Bees do it. Even educated fleas do it. So said Cole Porter about falling in love. To that we add:

> *Ice cream vendors in a good humor do it,*
> *Mechanics who twist a mean fender do it,*
> *Let's do it; let's rob us blind.*
> *The corner druggist we're told pill-fers,*
> *And the baker we know*
> *Kneads out a living,*
> *Stealing his own dough.*

Milking a business is a tradition, perfected to a high art by America's small businessmen. Perhaps this abuse speaks more eloquently of our insane tax laws than it does of our loss of Sunday School morality in the business community. Our tax laws are enough to drive any small businessman down the twisting road of rampant milking. Whatever school of economics you trust, you must agree that our tax structure punishes success: The more you make, the more Uncle Sam takes. As a result, America's businessmen have lived by the credo, "Better Me than Uncle Sam," for the past fifty years.

We do not intend to moralize here; I have no quarrel with any of these hard-working men. I do wonder, however, if all this feverish milking will merely deny the government a few bucks or whether, in the end, it will be the businessman and not the government who will be getting screwed.

I remember my friend Sidney's father, a pharmacist in the early 1950's, whose need to chisel Uncle Sam led to disaster.

Mr. Twyman ran a profitable little pharmacy, but filling prescriptions did not satisfy his need to make a fast buck. So he began to sell his own acne preparation in a little blue jar, the directions typed on the label. Word of Mr. Twyman's preparation spread around the neighborhood and soon there wasn't a kid on our block who didn't use "Tarex." What was this miracle formula? It was simply a coal-tar preparation concocted by a dermatologist friend of Twyman's in response to a request for something "stronger" than what was then commercially available for minor skin problems. Many local druggists were selling the same thing.

Tarex was no miracle product, but it was a good product. It worked in enough cases to build a growing number of users, and the neighborhood druggist's plain blue jar held greater attraction for the local population than a slick, mass-produced jar from a big company like Noxema. By the end of the year, business was so good that he had to clear a part of his basement exclusively for the production of Tarex.

Mr. Twyman began to itch for big money. He knew there were probably dozens of pharmacists making the same preparation and he wanted to beat them out at the marketplace. "Put it on the market," friends told him. "You'll be a millionaire." But the thought of preparing financial plans and business data for bankers or private lenders, of beginning a real factory with material and labor problems and complicated tax procedures turned him off. He was strictly a nickel-and-dime man. The compulsion to steal a tax-free dollar was far more intense than the one to earn a taxable thousand. So he decided to do it all himself.

He rented a small, dusty store a few blocks from his pharmacy and washed and scrubbed it until it was spotless. He equipped it with a primitive mixing vat, a few tables, some storage shelves, and a bunch of kids (myself included) who had free Saturday mornings. Then he found two pharmacy students to mix the stuff evenings and weekends. Every weekend thereafter, for six months, we sat sticking labels on blue jars of Tarex, "sold only at Twyman's Pharmacy." Mr. Twyman retained his brother-in-law, a lazy, jobless moocher, to peddle Tarex on a commission basis to other drug stores in Brooklyn. Tarex Pharmaceutical Company was born.

The shiftless brother-in-law proved a great salesman. He sold Tarex to over 150 stores in 8 weeks. And he continued, 2 months later pushing his way into Queens. Finally, emboldened by a day during which he had sold nearly 200 jars, he forayed into lower Manhattan and sold his first dozen jars to a pharmacist in Chinatown.

Mr. Twyman began to itch again. He was not content to stay in the pharmacy and wait for the sales reports. He was a pharmacist by profession but a retailer by trade, so he hired a pharmacist to spell him at the store and went out to sell the stuff himself.

Mr. Twyman drove us kids mercilessly. No matter how cockeyed the labels were or how much Tarex blobbed on the floor, he demanded more production. He had rented the store next door and there were now 10-foot stacks of jar cartons, three giant vats being stirred by pharmacy students, and three lines of teenage kids sticking on labels. Everybody in the neighborhood who passed the two black-windowed stores and peeked in to see this dazzling scene was convinced that Mr. Twyman was on his way to millions. But while business was booming, the checking balance was barely holding its own. Mr. Twyman had already begun his "one for you, two for me" bookkeeping system.

Twyman had found his system the first day out on the road when a greedy druggist offered him a deal. Tarex sold wholesale for 40¢ a jar for the small size, 60¢ for the medium size, and $1.20 for the popular, large size. Druggists turned it over at $1 for the small jar, $1.50 for the medium jar, and $2.50 for the large one. When the Bronx druggist learned that Twyman was the owner of Tarex, he offered him a deal. If Twyman would give the druggist another 10% off, he'd pay him cash. Twyman caught on and quickly agreed. Other druggists, hungry for higher profits on this popular item, accepted the deal and by the end of the day, nearly a third of all the sales Twyman had made were "samples, no charge." Lesson One in "Milkinomics."

Twyman had continued this practice, so while production and the number of nickels in his pockets were growing steadily, the company's net worth wasn't.

Twyman soon eliminated the charade of invoicing the cash sold goods as samples. He loaded his old Ford station wagon with cases of Tarex, ready to peddle the miracle of modern medicine like hot dogs off a cart. He had two price lists: one for cash with an extra 7% to 10% discount and one "on the books" at gross prices. While many customers preferred to pay the regular price and be invoiced, a significant minority liked the cash-and-carry deal. Twyman's off-the-books sales averaged $100 a week, which was no fortune but not exactly pennies, either, in 1953.

Twyman persisted in peddling until it became an out-and-out embarrassment. In 1956, he sold his store, expanded his "plant" into a full block front, and was not only making Tarex but about ten other "exes" for other pharmacies. He had been able to transform a good living as a retail pharmacist into a handsome one as a small, proprietary drug manufacturer in a few short years. He had no illusions about the potential of his product. There were dozens around just like it. There were bigger, smarter, faster people doing the same thing. So he decided to get the best out of what he had.

He sought out other small, fringe operators like himself with local preparations for coughs and rashes, baby oils, creams, and hair pomades and distributed them through his 1,000 customers in the metropolitan New York area. In 1957, he posted sales of $185,000 and probably did another $25,000 off the books. It was time to get off the road and inside to run the business. Twyman reluctantly agreed to come in from the cold in 1957, but his mind was still out there where all those delicious cash sales were. He spent endless, sleepless nights pacing the floor, trying to conjure other ways to keep his lucrative flow of cash moving.

The resourcefulness of a small businessman who wants to milk his business is boundless. It's been my opinion for years that a candy-store owner can find more ways to milk his business than the chief of a crime syndicate. With his mind firmly fixed on his objective, Twyman proceeded through the next 5 years to keep his company's bank balance manicured to size by these well-known but somewhat circuitous means:

1]   Twyman bought his jars from a small distributor. Rather than buy direct when his volume warranted large transactions with national glass companies, he continued buying his jars at a higher price because the jar man "worked with him." Here's what they did. The jar man sold Twyman a steady monthly order of jars. Every 3 months, he sent Twyman a phoney invoice for so many thousands of jars. Twyman promptly paid the invoice by check. The jar man deposited the check, drew 75% of the amount to his own name, cashed it and gave the cash to Twyman. These additional jars were shown in year-end statements as breakage, seconds, rejects, or as finished goods.

2]   Twyman borrowed sums of money from other suppliers, such as printers, chemical houses, and so forth. These loans were carried on the books over a period of time. When it suited him, Twyman "repaid" these loans to his colleagues who, in turn, turned the money back in cash to Twyman.

3]   Twyman added these people to the payroll:

     Sidney Twyman, Assistant Office Manager; $100 per week (My friend, aged 19, who attended college in Alabama)

     Dina Twyman, Inventory Clerk; $55 per week (Sidney's 14-year-old sister who attended Junior High School)

     Mildred Twyman, Office Manager; $125 per week (Twyman's wife who played canasta 7 days a week)

     Elsie Thatcher, Matron; $45 per week (Elsie was the Twyman's cleaning lady. Twyman split the $45 in half with her)

     Ben Twyman, Foreman; $175 per week (Twyman's 74-year-old father)

4]   Twyman rented the corner store to expand his

packing line, but when he noticed the pedestrian traffic passing the spot on weekends, he decided, instead, to open an "outlet store" for distressed pharmeceutical products—health and beauty aids purchased as job lots. He spent every Saturday for the next 7 years selling bruised Ex-Lax boxes to the constipated poor. For cash.

5] He sold all his own products, right out of inventory, for cash, in the store.

6] He began a "pickup" service for larger accounts at the factory where they paid cash.

7] Twyman wined and dined his family all over New York, Miami, Las Vegas, and Southern California on his way to or back from visits to "suppliers" or "prospects."

8] Twyman bought himself a new Cadillac every year as a "salesman's" car and bought a convertible for his wife, another for Sidney, and a fourth for the other salesman (his shiftless brother-in-law).

By 1959, Twyman grossed nearly $500,000 a year, mostly as a mass distributor of specialty nonprescription drug products. Tarex had long faded into well-deserved obscurity and re-emerged as "Empartex" skin lotion, a similarly small-volume but high-profit item. He now had 40 employees and had installed candy-vending machines for the packing girls along the walls behind the packing lines and Kotex machines in the ladies room. He split as much as $9 a week with the candy vendor, but the take from the Kotex machine, which he emptied after everyone went home at night, was all his. Naturally, having been a pharmacist he knew where to get Kotex wholesale.

One can now surmise that through these ploys and others too outrageous to even mention here, our friend was socking away big money. Exact figures can only be guessed at. Even Twyman's accountant claims to have been constantly baffled by his client's ability to scrape every last penny clean. However, we can take a fair guess at his annual average based on Twyman's own estimates (he is now happily out of the country).

Item	Twyman Grabbed
His Own Salary	$20,000
Legitimate Allowable Expenses	10,000
Padded Expenses	5,000
Padded Payroll	25,000
Phoney Purchases	10,000
Phoney Loans	3,000
Inventory Sold for Cash	15,000
Total Annual Take	88,000
Possible Legitimate Take	43,900
Taxable Milked Income	45,000
(including withholding for padded payroll)	
Legitimate Taxable Income	43,900
(had he drawn the money as a profit distribution)	
Actual Net Milk	43,000

If we assume the taxable income to reduce to the same net, then we can work with the presumed figure of $43,000 per year as the amount which Twyman milked out of his business. Over 7 years that comes to $301,000. There is no eighth year because, in 1964, Twyman went broke.

Before you conjure up any visions of this happy man departing for one of the lovely sunspots of the world with his $301,000 in hard, milked cash, let us report that this was not the case. Twyman had been forced to pour back all but about $35,000 of his money into the business during the years to save it from going under several times. While he happily milked away, his business remained dreadfully undercapitalized.

As the availability of low-cost filling and bottling machines forced him to automate, Twyman, had to go to his bank more than he should have. His chronically low balances in comparison to his volume suggested to his bankers that he was performing a larger-than-usual milk job, and they watched his credit carefully. They advanced him money little by little. He was forced to go outside regular channels to buy machinery. He found the interest rates in those channels understandably oppressive, so he began borrowing from his bank to repay the shylocks. Once having consolidated his debt back into legitimate channels, his machinery was again obsolete. New adapters and new handling equipment were desperately needed. He was now forced to dip into his own pocket to get them. Meanwhile, the neighborhood in which his small factory stood had deteriorated into a hopeless slum. Many of his key employees rebelled against coming to work in a high-crime area. He was forced to move quickly (something he should have done years before, but he didn't want to spend the money). He owed the bank too much. He wisely rejected the idea of going back to the shylocks. So he dipped into the personal sock again.

When his son graduated from the university and quickly married thereafter, Twyman had to begin actually allowing his son keep the payroll money while he attended law school. This was short lived. Soon Twyman needed the money, and when my friend actually needed the money, Twyman was forced to unpad his salary. My friend quit law school. He came to work for his father. He was back on the payroll at a higher salary because now his wife was pregnant.

During his first flush years, Twyman had acquired a summer house at a seaside area near New York. He bought furniture, rugs, plumbing, heating, and electrical contracting through the business. The company paid for everything. With the summer house came a widened social scope. Mrs. Twyman began entertaining like a grand society hostess. This ongoing quantum increase in Twyman's living cost was as much based on the yield of his business as it was on his capacity to continue milking his business. He was then forced to overdraw his own account to the extent that when a great opportunity came to expand profitably, he couldn't even raise the up-front money to begin.

A French maker of women's skin care products was looking for an East Coast distributor for a high-profit, well-established line with $500,000 in going volume for openers. The company management was willing to turn the line over to Twyman, providing he would support it by adding more salesmen and a larger warehouse facility to carry a large stock to service the trade and monies to expand the line throughout New England and the mid-Atlantic with advertising contributions. The price of this opportunity was about $75,000. Twyman's bank would not advance the money because he was already in too deep. His own resources had dwindled, and he refused to go into his own pocket for another dime. So he let the French line go to a competitor who later built it into an excellent, stable volume at a tremendous profit.

His "milking psychosis" had now deprived him of the chance to move into the million-dollar class. It had, in fact, kept him small.

It seems hard to believe that any man can be so blinded by cash greed that he'd let his business go down the drain just to protect his cash income. But it isn't. When receding sales and mordant policy finally reduced the company back down to deficit selling and Twyman declared himself bankrupt, his first instinct was to run to the store and sell out every last quarter's worth of stock at sacrifice prices so he could squeeze the last few hundred dollars out of his last days in business.

AUTOPSY

The premature demise of Mr. Twyman's business resulted from an attitude which began as a perfectly ordinary, understandable desire for a small businessman to skim a few bucks off the top but which evolved into an obsessive preoccupation with grabbing every dime in sight. Twyman never really understood the only real reason to be in business is to earn a profit and, by profit, to grow. As the years brought him a small measure of success, he willingly sacrificed the pursuit of an intelligent business objective to the idea of perpetuating the cow for the sake of milking it dry.

His decisions were deeply rooted in maintaining things as they were because, not unlike a reactionary politician, he was blindly concerned with maintaining status quo. Anything that threatened, or seemed to threaten, his comfortable weekly clutch of cash became abhorrent to him. He was forced into automating, forced into moving, forced into hiring every last employee whom he saw as a further depletion of his potential take.

Twyman's "cash" attitude so governed his mental processes that it became impossible to run a profitable business when inflation began trimming the fat off his margins. Instead of switching his jar business to a large national company who offered lower prices, he continued buying through a wholesaler and paying more, just to collar some cash. Instead of moving to newer quarters which would have enabled him to operate properly, he stayed too long in the cramped, dingy string of stores because he wanted to keep the outlet store and maintain a small, weekend, retail cash business.

Twyman was unquestionably an extreme case of a cash-crazy mentality. Chances are we all know one or two Twymans in our own communities who may be headed down the same road. There are probably hundreds of Twymans who have socked away millions with impunity. God knows there are enough legitimate, government-sanctioned, and, in some cases, blessed ways for a businessman to extract as much as possible out of his investment and labor over and above weekly draws or distribution of annual profits. Today, it's better to go by the book than to chance running afoul of the Byzantine tax laws for what is really never more than a piddling amount of cash. Great fortunes in business were nearly always made by massive aboveboard movements of capital, merchandise, or stocks. Cash mentalities produce tips. If you want to live on tips, you should be a waiter or drive a cab.

What is worst about overmilking your business is not the hypocrisy, but the sheer stupidity of keeping a business cash poor. Since the Government began its count, the single largest cause of small-business failure has been undercapitalization. Today in capital-greedy, inflated America, it's downright suicide to be cash poor. Having lots of money in your business gives you the kind of heft and leverage against anything that comes your way that nothing else can replace.

Cash gives you a mighty hammer at the bank.

Cash gives you clout with your suppliers. A man who pays his bills on time gets the best prices and deliveries most of the time.

Cash gives you the flexibility to reward your employees, boost morale, invest when opportunity comes, expand when you want to, and meet competition. Most of all, cash gives you a sense of security; come what may, your chances of riding out an unforeseen storm are doubly good.

This is not to suggest that you simply dump all your cash

into the business. But it does suggest that you should take a periodic, hard look at your cash position in relation to your sales, your inventory, and your own remuneration. It further prods you into thinking through your greed. You shouldn't deny your greed. It's natural. If you weren't greedy, you wouldn't be in business. A healthy, controlled appetite to accumulate and wisely spend more money is nothing to be ashamed of.

But running away with yourself at first temptation will surely set you on a nutty course trod by all the small-minded men who squirrel away each milked-out buck in the hopes of denying more and more to Uncle Sam. It is not so much a question of grabbing or not grabbing as it is a question of how much grabbing is being done at the expense of what. People somehow fail to appreciate the simple fact that regardless of whether they are stealing from Uncle Sam or simply stealing from themselves, they are perpetrating a theft, nonetheless, which is not without consequences. If you make a cash sale for $500 and split it with your partner, you think you've grabbed the whole $500. But you haven't. You've grabbed the difference between the $500 and the cost of what you sold—let us say $150. You split $150, therefore, or $75 each. What would you do with the $75? Donate it to heart research? No. You're human. You'd probably buy one $15 tie, take your wife out for a $35 dinner, and throw the rest away on junk like banana-shaped transistor radios.

We presume there are many who'd damn well know better things to do with cash proceeds than buy banana-shaped radios. But if you really search your mind, you'll find that we are a trinket-loving society and that most of the milking done in small business does, in fact, wind up buying trinkets. It's awfully tough to lay down big money for personal investment on milked funds.

If you're a more prudent milker than Twyman, good man! But we remain cynical. Based on my observations, it makes a helluva lot more sense to give yourself a big, fat raise than diddle out tips to yourself.

After all, who the hell is the boss anyway?
Who?

10

Selling Your Business Down the River

Y O U   W A K E up one morning, and before you've finished shaving, the same miserable day you had yesterday is already forming in your head. Apex is still pressing for their order. You can't fill it. The bank wants your new financials before they okay the extended credit line you requested. Your accountant is on a pink beach in Jamaica, frolicking with his kids in the sun. You ask yourself, "Why aren't I frolicking with my kids in the sun?"

But it's time to go. You've sat too long on the toilet bowl. You'll miss your train. You pass up breakfast again. You take the car instead of taking a late train. You broil up a temper sitting in choking traffic. You arrive at work ready to tear everyone's head off. The morning's order mail is thin. Where are all your salesmen? What the hell are they doing?

Your production man rushes frenetically through your door. The number #34 Lickety splitting machine, won't split. Tons of materials are stacked up on the receiving dock, but your receiving manager is busy yakking to his ex-wife about overdue alimony payments. That means he'll be in about a raise any minute.

You try to call Chicago. You can't get through. Their operator doesn't understand your operator. A man from Detroit is here to look over the place. You'd forgotten that appointment. You waste half the day showing him how nothing works while your plant manager tears out his hair waiting to talk to you about the boys in the machine shop who have threatened a wildcat strike after lunch.

You work late again. As you walk across the parking lot to

your car, a punk eases up behind you, raps you one across the head, grabs your wallet, and leaves you dripping blood across your sweated brow. Well, thank God, it's Friday.

Tomorrow is Saturday. You have your choice. If its sunny, you can have the pleasure of listening to all your boring friends telling boring stories at the boring club again. If its lousy, you can take the kids to the movies and watch Charlie Brown amid a sea of 500 screaming, candy-munching, rotten children. Then you can come home and listen to your wife complain about all the time you never seem to have for her.

Is this what the hell it's all about, you ask? What is this witch's brew I've managed to concoct that conspires to put me through a meat-grinder every day, rob me of my humanity, and turn my family into demanding tyrants?

So you wake up the following Monday morning. You call your accountant who is home from frolicking in Jamaica. You tell him you are goddamn fed up with the worries, the sleepless nights, the endless hours, and the persistent terror of managing a small, growing business. You tell him you want to sell.

Let someone else have the headaches.

Let someone else take everyone else's crap.

Let me get my money and run fast to another company where someone else has the nightmares, and I can collect a nice corporate salary, fly in the company jet, spend my evenings with my family, and my weekends on the shores of a rushing stream where the trout leap out of the water and the skies are not cloudy all day.

You've got plenty of good reasons to sell. But there arc bad reasons too.

If you sell for the right reasons, you've given new life to yourself. If you sell for the wrong reasons or at the wrong time, you are robbing yourself of something very special in your life and, in effect, murdering the business itself. Its tough to recognize what's right at the time, and no matter what you decide, you will probably eat your heart out anyway.

This chapter tries to point out one aspect of this conundrum that is very common. It's about killing a part of yourself by selling your business when you shouldn't.

Emanual and Abraham Dohri, two immigrants from Istanbul, established a basement speciality bakery in the Bronx, New York, just before World War I. They sold wafer cookies to candy stores and later manufactured ice cream cones from an ancient machine. They worked for 25 years, coming up to the surface floor and then to their own above-street-level plant, emerging with a modestly successful enterprise—baking ice cream cones for most beaches, parks, and public amusement areas in the greater New York area.

The Dohri brothers' volume breakthrough came in 1939, when the New York World's Fair opened in Flushing Meadow. By underbidding New York's largest bakers in a bold, lowball shot, they gained entrée to supply all the cones for the fair's ice cream stands. This provided a quantum leap in sales with a small dollar loss but incalculable promotional value in the trade that paid immense dividends later on. Not long after the fair closed, the Big Top Cone Company was the dominant factor in the New York market.

Right after World War II, they moved to a larger bakery with triple the capacity. Realizing they could no longer exist as a one-product house, they turned to their head baker, Armand, whose primitive genius for tinkering produced a simple machine which produced cheese sandwich snacks. They retained their first commission sales representatives and watched, with immense satisfaction, the slowly but surely building list of customers in the grocery trade. The two salesmen aggressively pursued the market, battling for outlets street by street, the way soldiers take a town. Big Top sales climbed higher as representatives from Philadelphia, Boston, and the Baltimore/Washington area began opening up accounts. By 1952, there was sufficient rolling volume for the firm to move into a renovated, four-story, 100,000-square-foot building into which they moved their bakery.

Spurred by the encouraging cheers of their fathers, Henry Dohri and James Dohri now took over the business. Both young men, filled with moxie, brains, and that singular mixture of sophistication and common sense otherwise known as piss and vinegar were in their late twenties; time and the world was before them. Henry assumed overall administrative responsibilities, while James undertook to learn, at Armand's side, the production side of the business. They built a national network of sales representatives, who helped them create a family of distributors, servicing hundreds of thousands of grocery stores and supermarkets all over America. They'd grown from a two-product house to a ten-product house, now selling bagged snack products like cheese puffs and corn chips.

These products placed Big Top on a gigantic field facing formidable competitors. They were one of a small handful of independent operators in a business of giants. To maintain their position, it was necessary to build consumer recognition of the Big Top brand. But the Dohris had neither the capital or the inclination to mortgage the bakery for a program of consumer advertising. Yet Henry Dohri felt his company could not sit back on its share of market and simply hope for the best. If he could not spend enough TV dollars to make consumers hear his name with a thunderous voice, he could make it seem like a thundrous voice to the other people who counted—the trade.

By adroit manipulation of a minimal budget of TV advertising on morning children's television programs, Henry and his marketing staff were able to make a $150,000 budget sound like $2 million. They merely inundated the trade magazines and distributor organizations with a torrent of literature featuring photos of celebrated children's TV characters, huge blocks of type screaming gigantic numbers of audiences—imparting the clear impression to the trade that Big Top was big time. The Dohris didn't create this device, it was older than Henry Dohri himself. But it worked.

The Dohris also tightened the cordon around their organization by running continuous sales meetings around the country with their representatives and distributors. These meetings became, after some years, semifamily gatherings in tone; but the Big Top staff put together an endless flow of highly creative promotions which sent the Big Top people out for bear every time.

All this drive, all this energy, was bound to send vibrations throughout the food industry, especially to the large corporations which dominated the grocery manufacturing field. Big Top sales had reached $10,000,000 in 1965. Less than twenty years before, sales were under $1 million. The Dohris had done their work well, but the pace at which they were now running began demanding too much. They began to sputter now and then. And while both Henry and James possessed a uniformly even-tempered intelligence, we can assume that their normally sensible, even placid, attitudes were beginning to shrivel in the heat of expansion. Now perhaps, some of those blue mornings began creeping up on them.

Henry Dohri's blue funks were undoubtedly embedded in his growing restiveness with running a family business and working overtime to handle all the headaches involved, instead of being an executive making big decisions and rushing off to the club for lunch. The nitty-gritty of the business, he felt, was a waste of his time and talent. The thought of selling the business had occurred to him with increasing frequency over the past 3 years. Not for the money. He was already rather comfortable. But as a means of escape, a chance to enter that corporate world 50 stories high where men wore $500 suits and gravely discussed the movements of unimaginable sums of money. He didn't want to go to his grave as another immigrant's son who'd made money in the food business. His malaise turned to a turbulent discontent with what he now felt were the dull chores of running the business each day. It was on one of those fretful Monday mornings in the spring of 1965 that he met a top corporate staff man from Amalgamated Dairy & Food at an industry seminar.

Amalgamated was a billion-dollar corporation whose top management had recently been shaken to the toes to pump blood into its sagging, flaccid old body. Its traditional dairy business was unprofitable; many of its diversifications had been ill-advised. But it had a treasury laden with coin, most of which had been made over the company's 100-year history delivering milk to millions of American homes in a familiar yellow van.

The new executive team was determined to diversify ADF into the higher-profit processed food and snack manufacturing fields. Snack foods was a particular area of interest because industry figures showed that more people were sitting in front of the television set gobbling snacks than ever, and their numbers were increasing every year. ADF's idea was to assemble a group of small snack food and related confectionery companies into a group profit center which could be expanded by acquisition until it made up $150,000,000 in annual volume, or 15% of the ADF total.

As Harmon Hadley, the ADF man, related these broad plans to Henry, he continually referred to Big Top as the "type of company" which would "fit into the ADF plan." Henry asked Hadley on the spot whether ADF was beckoning. Hadley admitted Big Top had been under study for 6 months and that he had planned to "accidently bump into" Henry at the seminar to discuss his ideas.

At a follow-up lunch, Henry and James met ADF's Chairman and President. They confirmed that ADF wanted Big Top. They pointed out that an all-cash deal was fine with them, but that if they wanted part of their money in the blue chip ADF stock, that could be arranged too. Henry and James took the results of their meeting back to the company. Their fathers, long retired, agreed to abide by anything the two cousins wanted. Other family members who held company stock also agreed to abide by the Dohris' decision, whether yes or no.

Now Henry and James began that agonizing process of decision-making through which so many businessmen have gone: to sell or not to sell.

Selling to ADF at the price informally discussed, or anything within its range, would transform all the Dohris into millionaires. Yet this consideration, while central, was not the emotional trigger that set in motion the final decision. The real appeal of the ADF offer lay in its personal aspects.

During the preliminary negotiations, Hadley's flattery and admiration for the two dynamic Dohris added a new dimension to the deal. ADF not only needed companies like Big Top, they needed young managers like Henry and James Dohri. Hadley told the Dohris that a new horizon awaited them within the ADF family. There was that great leap forward sense about Hadley's offer. There they were, sons of Turkish immigrants—hard working and well educated, but never before candidates for the great board rooms of America. It almost seemed too good. But Hadley came through; along with an offer of $3,000,000 for the business, there was the offer of a position as Group Vice President of the entire Processed Snack Division of ADF for Henry Dohri and for James, the succession as President and Chief Executive Officer of

the Big Top Division of ADF. The Dohris decided. It was go.
The acquisition of Big Top Snacks, Inc. was completed in
early 1966. Henry Dohri left his modest office on the second floor
of the old Big Top bakery in a seedy industrial district of New
York for a plush office at ADF corporate headquarters on New
York's Madison Avenue. The exhaltation of the fantastic personal challenge ahead coursed through Henry's veins like
adrenaline through an Olympic athlete preparing for a dash for
the Gold Medal. Henry built a magnificent new home on Long
Island's Gold Coast and settled in to master the domain he
thought lay before him.

While Henry now sat like a sultan in the movie, *Lawrence of
Arabia,* James faced the Perils of Pauline. One of the central
benefits of membership in big-time corporate America was access
to capital. Big Top now called the markers and ADF was not
wanting. Cramped, bursting, and chronically underproduced in
its old plant, Big Top laid plans for a new one. With the firm
financial support of ADF, Big Top went ahead and built a tremendous snack bakery, spanking new with double its existing capacity, and a year later, the new Big Top plant was completed. As
Henry handed the symbolic key to his cousin, he remarked in a
telling aside, "Now we can finally make everything we want. The
trick now, is to sell it all."

James set to work shaking down the plant with his characteristic energy and quiet aplomb. No sooner had the machines
started and the ovens been fired up, however, than an army of
gremlins attacked the plant, making every production problem
seem ten times worse. Wrapping machines didn't wrap, ovens
didn't bake, raw materials arrived late, pilferage ran wild, there
were labor problems, computer errors, and massive foul-ups in
production scheduling. When the trade was screaming for Corn
Twistiedoos, Big Top was making Pizzaroodles, which were coming back from the trade by the ton because they weren't selling.

Many of these problems are de rigeur in any new plant
shakedown. But there was a far more grave problem bubbling
beneath the managerial surface. Under Henry's leadership, Big
Top could afford to be price-independent because it sold as
much as it could make in the old, overcrowded plant. Henry
looked good. Once Big Top moved into an expensive new plant,

in which it could produce nearly double of what they were then selling, the signals changed. James looked bad. Executives at Big Top didn't make this obvious assumption. They preferred to assume that had Henry remained at Big Top, things would have been different. They already had their eye on Big Daddy downtown. They weren't working for Big Top anymore. They were already working for ADF in mind and spirit.

Henry had done a beautiful job coping with the old, obsolete plant and maintaining a high level of corporate efficiency. But he had failed in one important task. He failed to properly prepare James to assume the leadership in a crisis situation. Perhaps it simply was not in his mind as he prepared for his own destiny in the board rooms of Madison Avenue.

James now began asking direct questions.

Whose assumption was it that Big Top should be operating like a ticking little Swiss watch bare months after it opened?

Whose assumption was it that doubled production capacity could be filled by doubled sales within the first year?

He found out quickly. When the honeymoon was over, the bottom line was this: ADF gave you a new plant. You make twice as much. You sell twice as much. You have a nice, fat figure to show on the bottom line as a contribution to corporate profits. That's the assumption. And there's one other. If you can't do it, Jack, we'll find someone who can.

With this background, 1967 and 1968 passed in a perpetual state of peril for James. He constantly sought solace and advice from Henry, who complied to the best of his ability. But Henry's head was now in another place; he was above the daily skirmishes with the gremlins—sunk in a sea of figures, charts, projections, and an endless series of cross-country jaunts in the corporate jet. Henry could no longer relate to the late arrival of corn meal, or a cello wrapper that didn't cello wrap. Everyone at the plant now sensed that James was totally on his own, and Henry confirmed it.

James now burrowed in to grapple with his problems. When Big Top was a family fief, profits were something they had to explain either existed or didn't exist every year after the board meeting when Aunt Emma asked about them. Now it wasn't Aunt Emma anymore; it was those tens of thousands of Aunt Emmas who held ADF stock who expected their executive team to produce big dividends.

So James continued the struggle to run Big Top as sparely and leanly as possible. He'd come under the ADF corporate umbrella with two big strikes against him. First, the obligation to make the new plant pay within a reasonable time; second, to amortize that new, monster production capacity profitably. And in the background was the deepening process of amalgamation of the newly acquired ten snack companies into one big division.

James acquired and dispensed with several key sales and marketing executives during this time. Under private ownership, executive changes were about as frequent as snowstorms in Santa Fe. Now sheer parent company profit pressure, not James, not Henry, was running Big Top. James soon undertook virtually the entire executive burden himself, assisted only by one, loyal, resilient man who served him as marketing director.

The two men drove themselves twelve to fifteen hours a day building sales, producing more items, cutting budgets to Spartan levels, making nearly all central decisions themselves. As the numbers game dominated their conscious thoughts, it soon obsessed them. They finally examined the result of a year's grueling labor one late evening. It was good, but not good enough.

So once again, out came the long knives. A merciless analysis of selling costs resulted in the mass discharge of the 35-year-old sales commission brokerage organization. Corporate management wanted to share sales expenses over three snack divisions selling similar product lines. Many of the representatives discharged had labored tirelessly for Big Top over 25 years or more. Such sudden dismissals were certainly understandable in corporate terms. But the question we must ask is: Would this have happened under private management? Thus old familiar faces disappeared and Big Top was reduced, finally, from an independent, sharply focused corporate presence to a drone plant of a great corporation.

Personnel cuts continued unabated. ADF was determined to make Big Top profitable at any cost because so many other companies they'd bought had turned out to be such impossible clinkers. The burden thus fell on fewer shoulders.

Finally, in 1970, ADF let the other shoe drop. It announced

the integration of Big Top into the Sayer's Foods Group, a larger producer of snack and confectionery products in the ADF family. Big Top was assimilated as a brand of Sayer's. The Big Top plant became ADF #130 NY.

In a further economy move spurred by miserable corporate performance, ADF decided to evacuate its posh Manhattan towers and move its international corporate headquarters to its prime production facility in the South. Henry Dohri, who had been quietly advancing in top corporate ranks, was then confronted by the decision to either move south or leave Amalgamated. The company wanted Henry to move, but Henry suddenly spurned his newly won status as a corporate man. He refused a generous offer to move and decided, instead, to take his chances in his hometown. Life had taken a strange turn for Henry Dohri. A dream achieved, a place arrived at, instead of looking like an Elysian Field, resembled a vast wasteland. He reluctantly submitted his resignation to the board in June 1970. James Dohri, realizing his own status had, in effect, been reduced from a Divisional President to a Plant Manager, followed Henry out within 6 months.

These two cousins, who had presided with intelligence, grace, and vigor over the maturation of a family firm, had large stacks of ADF shares to provide physical comforts for a lifetime, but felt empty-handed. Henry Dohri took time off to travel around the world for 3 months. He'd planned to return to corporate life or, perhaps, consider public service when he returned. A few tepid offers were tendered, but nothing Henry saw as sufficiently challenging to jar him from the growing dilettantism of early middle age. Indulging a recurring passion for scholarly pursuit, he began a serious study of religious mysticism as his commercial impulses faded with each passing day in the relaxed security of his library. James Dohri traveled too, played tennis and golf, toyed with a few ideas, met a lot of people for lunch, and fell asleep at boring avant-garde plays. Both men are personally adrift on a golden boat on a calm sea, no threatening storms forcing them to shore. Yet a sense of loss and resignation surrounds them. One is tempted to think about whether they lay awake at night thinking how life would be had they not sold Big Top.

Although it makes its contribution, hidden in some pennies per share in ADF's annual dividend, Big Top is dead as a company, as a corporate personality, as a vivid thing in the lives of the men who made it.

A U T O P S Y

The Dohris sold Big Top for damn good reasons. They received a big bagful of money and stock. They are all financially secure for life. But men sell their companies for other reasons, as we said in the beginning. Perhaps a man's son prefers contemplation on a Himalayan Peak with an Indian mystic to wholesaling Number Nine Lickety Splits. It may break his father's heart to see the business go to seed for want of an heir, so the guy sells. Okay. A business may need capital it can't raise itself. It may need financial and management leverage. Okay. That's a good reason to sell. But remember, a guy who sells a business he likes is selling more than assets listed on a piece of paper. He's selling part of himself. That's what the Big Top story is about.

Is the money the Dohris got enough to pay for the change in their lives, their attitudes toward their futures as men? That's what this discussion is about. A man should not only take a long, hard look at what a buyer is offering; he should consider how selling will change that which he values most—his sense of self. No amount of money or stock is enough to pay for the pride some men feel arising each morning and working at something they love.

The haters may be genuine haters, and they, by all means, ought to get out as soon as possible. I know such a man. He hated what he was doing. He cursed and spattered spittle all over his shirt every day. He detested the long hours, the relentless pace. He found his colleagues boring and his customers boorish. He continued lengthening his vacations and business trips. The business had been left to him by his father, and having no other way of making it during the Depression, he had gone into it, been swallowed up, and run down into a bitter middle age. All he had to look forward to was more of the same. This prospect terrified him.

When he began grinding his teeth in his sleep, he knew he was coming to the end of the road. A larger firm in the field had been after him for years. But they'd lowballed him. Then, suddenly, in the early stages of an expansion, they called him, quoting the same low offer. His lawyers and accountants shrugged it off as ridiculous again. But he didn't. What *was* "ridiculous" to him was grinding his teeth at night and hating half his conscious moments. He took the offer. It was 25% below fair market value at the time. But he cared little. He wanted to buy freedom.

Months later, when he had completed the sale and was cheerfully engaged carving wood sculpture in a studio behind his house, he related why he sold out so cheap. "I'd never be here," he said. "I'd still be down there spilling my guts on the floor every day. I had an offer. I was so desperate to get out, I think I would have taken it all in bubble gum. The $100,000, well, yes, I threw it away. But it was the best money I ever spent. That hundred grand bought me back my life. And that is cheap, my friend."

No contest.

Our glimpse into the lives of the Dohris, in contrast, points to another case. When Big Top was sold, both Dohris were in their early to middle forties. Both enjoyed fine health. Both were capable, by any measure, of steering the company into new paths of glory all alone. Yet the siren call of the board room overshadowed the personal considerations. They envisioned a great challenge in their future with ADF. And besides, there was always the reminder of *all that money.*

But how can any businessman put a price tag on contentment, serenity, a sense of command, and control of one's life? When a buyer waves big money in your face, you can resist to a point. Sooner or later, visions of those stacks of money get you drunk. That's the time to sober up. Take a few weeks. Alone. Don't think about the money; you've already done that. Don't think about your wife, or kids, or estate, or taxes, or employees, or friends. Think about yourself. You, above them all, are the most important reason to sell or to hold, assuming, of course, no special duress exists.

If you love your business and the work you do, and you can't think of anything else you'd like better, except maybe to make some more money—hold off. Stay put. Stand pat. Spend your energies seeking ways to make more money in the business as it is now. Bear in mind, no matter who may buy you out, no matter how nice they seem, no matter how much your mutual aspirations seem mated in heaven, things will change.

Don't feel guilty if, by refusing a juicy offer, you deprive your family of a new world of instant, insane luxury or impossibly secure, long-range wealth. If you've been a good mother or father, if you've loved and understood your family and they you, that's good enough. You don't owe your personal happiness to a preconceived notion as to how much happier your family might be sailing across the Country Club inlet in a 60-foot cabin cruiser. Don't sell out your life for anything on this earth, including your family.

By all means, sell to a bigger outfit if you want more personal scope within a good management contract. But be sure you've evacuated all deep emotions about what may happen to your business after you no longer own it. Remember, if you're going along with the package, you'll bear witness.

If you think you've got better things to do with your mind, your generous heart, and your remaining time on earth than continuing to sell the same dull products to the same dull people year in and year out, by all means, get out. Now what will you do with that liberated life of yours? Will you build a fireplace in your living room? Will you plant prize-winning begonias? Will you teach at Sunday school? Know that before and begin getting your head into it early. Then, once you are free, forget you ever saw a profit-and-loss statement.

It's been my experience that most men who sell businesses like to start new businesses more attuned to their personal needs. That's good and healthy. So if you've always liked to paint, you could think about becoming an artist, but there's nothing wrong with opening a local art gallery either.

Selling a business is like marrying off a child. If it's been obnoxious, boorish, snide, rotten, and ungrateful, you should be glad to get rid of it. If, on the other hand, you love it and cherish it, take care how you hand it over and to whom you hand it over.

Remember.

It's yours.

In Memoriam

O N T H E T O P of the hill at Mount Hardluck Cemetery sit the graves of our company owners. Perched on their tombstones, our heroes listen to each other's tragic tales with disbelief.

Wayne the Beef King can't believe that Twyman would steal money from his own drug business and the Internal Revenue Service. "That's unpatriotic!" Wayne sobs, dusting off the American flag planted next to his grave.

"I don't see how you couldn't smell a phoney the minute he set foot in your office, Steve," says Medway's former owner. Harry, the advertising genius, is too busy checking to make sure that the caretakers are weeding the expensive tulips in his plot to even listen to the others.

They sit there discussing common business problems, longing for another chance to make that big deal they missed. But it is not to be. Buried with them are the rubble and ruin of their wasted little empires, which will keep them company for an eternity during which they will have plenty of time to ask themselves, *Why me?*

What lessons have their failures provided for the rest of us, who may be pleasantly coasting toward similar destruction without knowing it?

Ask yourself these questions:

What are the reasons you went into business? Are they the same reasons you are staying in business?

Is there someone in your company who thinks he knows more than you, is better than you and commands more loyalty from your key customers and employees than you do? If so, is it healthy or unhealthy?

Are you having delusions of grandeur because you've just gone public?

Can you resist a wild scheme to make big money?

Can your company survive if your production man walks out?

How often did you kid yourself this week?

Do you really feel a sense of control? Who's running the business?

Stare truth in the face. Of course it's tough. Making believe a harsh fact of business life doesn't exist is always a snap. It's not easy to force yourself to admit that you make stupid mistakes. It's easier to blame someone else. But once you adopt the habit, you may even get so good at facing facts that you'll recognize potential mistakes before you make them and save yourself money, aggravation, and maybe the business itself.

Running a profitable small business is a state of mind. Success is something nobody can talk you into. Or out of. The important fact to remember is that small companies are more sensitive to the insanities of ownership than large public corporations and they must be watched much more carefully.

If you feel, in your heart of hearts, that you are bored, or tired, or disillusioned, or indifferent or just plain unhappy owning, working for, or running your small business—get out. Everything depends on what you want. *If it's worth it to you to invest your time, your money, your health and your years in your business, it will be worth it to understand that your business is no different from your body. If you take care of it, it will take care of you.*

So do things sensibly, logically and humanly. Subject your judgments to the continuing evaluation of your common sense. Make your blunders. Screw up from time to time as you must. But keep diagnosing every two weeks, every month.

A balance-sheet bottom line is not the *real* bottom line.